JOHN MAIN

MODERN SPIRITUAL MASTERS
Robert Ellsberg, Series Editor

This series introduces the writing and vision of some of the great spiritual masters of the twentieth century. Along with selections from their writings, each volume includes a comprehensive introduction, presenting the author's life and writings in context and drawing attention to points of special relevance to contemporary spirituality.

Some of these authors found a wide audience in their lifetimes. In other cases recognition has come long after their deaths. Some are rooted in long-established traditions of spirituality. Others charted new, untested paths. In each case, however, the authors in this series have engaged in a spiritual journey shaped by the influences and concerns of our age. Such concerns include the challenges of modern science, religious pluralism, secularism, and the quest for social justice.

At the dawn of a new millennium this series commends these modern spiritual masters, along with the saints and witnesses of previous centuries, as guides and companions to a new generation of seekers.

Already published:
Dietrich Bonhoeffer (edited by Robert Coles)
Simone Weil (edited by Eric O. Springsted)
Henri Nouwen (edited by Robert A. Jonas)
Pierre Teilhard de Chardin (edited by Ursula King)
Anthony de Mello (edited by William Dych, S.J.)
Charles de Foucauld (edited by Robert Ellsberg)
Oscar Romero (by Marie Dennis, Rennie Golden,
    and Scott Wright)
Eberhard Arnold (edited by Johann Christoph Arnold)
Thomas Merton (edited by Christine M. Bochen)
Thich Nhat Hanh (edited by Robert Ellsberg)
Rufus Jones (edited by Kerry Walters)
Mother Teresa (edited by Jean Maalouf)
Edith Stein (edited by John Sullivan, O.C.D.)

Forthcoming volumes include:
Mohandas Gandhi
Flannery O'Connor
G. K. Chesterton

MODERN SPIRITUAL MASTERS SERIES

JOHN MAIN

Essential Writings

Selected
with an Introduction by
LAURENCE FREEMAN

ORBIS BOOKS

Maryknoll, New York 10545

Founded in 1970, Orbis Books endeavors to publish works that enlighten the mind, nourish the spirit, and challenge the conscience. The publishing arm of the Maryknoll Fathers and Brothers, Orbis seeks to explore the global dimensions of the Christian faith and mission, to invite dialogue with diverse cultures and religious traditions, and to serve the cause of reconciliation and peace. The books published reflect the views of their authors and do not represent the official position of the Maryknoll Society. To learn more about Maryknoll and Orbis Books, please visit our website at www.maryknoll.org.

Library of Congress Cataloging-in-Publication Data

Main, John, O.S.B.
    John Main : essential writings / selected with an introduction by Laurence Freeman.
        p. cm. – (Modern spiritual masters series)
    Includes bibliographical references.
    ISBN 1-57075-415-2 (pbk.)
    1. Spiritual life – Catholic Church. 2. Meditation – Catholic Church.
I. Freeman, Laurence. II. Title. III. Series.
BX2350.3 .M25 2002
248.4'82 – dc21

                                                    2002000674

Contents

Sources

AW   *Awakening: On Retreat with John Main* (London: Medio Media, 1997).

BW   *Being on the Way*, tapes (London: Medio Media, 1991).

CL   *Community of Love* (London: Darton, Longman & Todd, 1990; New York: Continuum, 1999).

CM   *Christian Meditation: The Gethsemani Talks* (London: Medio Media, 1999).

FA   *Fully Alive*, tapes (London: Medio Media, 1991).

HC   *The Heart of Creation* (London: Darton, Longman & Todd, 1988; New York: Continuum, 1998).

IC   *The Inner Christ* (London: Darton, Longman & Todd, 1987).

LH   *Letter from the Heart* (New York: Crossroad, 1982).

MC   *Moment of Christ* (London: Darton, Longman & Todd, 1984).

PC   *The Present Christ* (London: Darton, Longman & Todd, 1985; New York: Crossroad, 1985).

WMF   *Word Made Flesh* (London: Darton, Longman & Todd, 1993; New York: Continuum, 1998).

WS   *Word into Silence* (London: Darton, Longman & Todd, 1980; New York: Paulist Press, 1981).

WU   *Way of Unknowing* (London: Darton, Longman & Todd, 1989; New York: Crossroad, 1989).

Grateful acknowledgment is made to the publishers cited above and to the World Community for Christian Meditation.

Chronology of John Main

1926	January 21. Born in London
1931	Enrolled at St. Mary's Parochial School, Hendon
1932	School for one year in Ballinskelligs, County Kerry, Ireland
1933–37	Resumed schooling in London
1937	Scholarship to Westminster Cathedral Choir School
1939–42	St. Ignatius School, Welwyn Garden City
1942	Cub journalist with the *Hornsey Journal*, North London
1943	Enlisted with the Royal Corps of Signals, served in Belgium and France
1946	Novice with Canons Regular in Cornwall
1949	Studied with Canons Regular in Rome
1950–54	Law School at Trinity College, Dublin
1955–56	British Colonial Service in Malaya
1956–58	Taught Law at Trinity College, Dublin
1958	Death of nephew David
1959	Entered Ealing Abbey, London
1960–62	Studied at San Anselmo, Rome, Italy
1962	Solemn Profession as monk
1963	Ordained priest at Ealing

1963–69   Second Master at St. Benedict's School, Ealing

1969–74   Headmaster, St. Anselm's School, Washington, D.C.

1975   Returned to London, founded first Meditation
          Centre and lay community

1976   Gave retreat at Gethsemani Abbey, Kentucky

1977   Founded Benedictine Priory of Montreal

1978   Publication of *Word into Silence* and *Christian
          Meditation: The Gethsemani Talks*

1979   Operation for cancer

1981   Publication of *Letters from the Heart*

1982   Wrote foreword to *Moment of Christ*
          December 30. Died in Montreal

Introduction

John Main once claimed that his essential teaching could be written on the back of a postage stamp. It will take a little more space than that to explain what he meant.

Because his is a spiritual teaching, indeed a mystical one, it cannot be adequately described in the way we would explain a philosophy or theology. It asks to be understood at a personal level, where thought and experience, mind and heart, converge. It was from the depth of his own personal integration that his teaching emerged. Nevertheless this teaching has far-reaching ramifications into many modern religious and social concerns. As a spiritual teacher John Main directly addresses modern doubt and dread with the insights and experience of a mature Christian faith — one that is both true to tradition and radically modern.

Theologians have called John Main a "Trinitarian mystic." For Bede Griffiths he was "the best spiritual guide in the church today." The Dalai Lama has expressed his admiration for this fellow monk who taught meditation from the Christian tradition. This anthology of John Main presents his message as he delivered it in written or spoken word during a short five-year period, ending with his death in 1982. But his ongoing influence is now embedded in the global community he inspired. And his impact on the inner silence of those who still meet him through his words is, as ever, essentially personal and direct.

I have organized the following selections in categories introduced by a short commentary on his thought in those areas. His teaching is clear, simple, never merely speculative. And it has the practical aim of leading people from thought to experience, from words to silence. You finally understand him only in the light of your experience of meditation. Here I will offer a sketch of the man as I knew him. Understanding his life helps us appreciate the link between life and teaching that characterizes all true masters.

•

I first met John Main in 1963, when at the age of twelve I was sitting in a classroom of boys eagerly awaiting the first appearance of our new religion teacher. Having accomplished our ruthless destruction of his predecessor's self-confidence, we were eager to see if we could perform the same service to "Brother John." All we knew was that he was a monk, but not yet a priest, which, of course for Catholics, made him an easier victim. The school bell rang, silence fell in the corridors, and we listened as his footsteps approached. A tall, slim monk in a Benedictine habit entered the room and closed the door. He turned and looked at us looking at him, appraising us with a smiling self-confidence that instantly made us realize that he would be no victim of ours. We were immediately his pupils. His authority was natural, not assumed. He betrayed none of the usual schoolmaster's fear of losing control. With the quick intuition of children we sensed an unusual authenticity of personality. We were charmed, however, rather than dominated by his strong presence. We were also surprised to find a teacher who, while certainly having something to say, seemed to treat us as equals or at least as capable of equality. What I can remember from the term he taught this class was his theme of worshiping the true God rather than the idols of consumer materialism — reality over illusion, as he would later put it. This was the new Vatican II theology we were receiving. Having been reared on insular Catholicism, catechism, and dogma, this was for us a new approach to religion altogether: enlightening rather than indoctrinating.

Although a day school, St. Benedict's preserved some traits of the public school culture that it inherited from Downside Abbey, its founding community. At lunch in those days the boys would sit at long tables with a master at the head. I and a small group of my friends enjoyed being at John Main's table, where we had animated conversation with him about grownup subjects, and we were often pleased to be shocked by his liberal views on church and politics. We felt flattered by the attention he gave even to our usually more conservative opinions. He made us think. The difficulty of believing some of the things he said made the conversation all the more challenging. He once surprised us by claiming that as a child in Ireland he used to walk barefoot across the fields to school. Even more surprisingly to our middle-class Catholic minds, he saw no reason not to have an atheist who was a good man as prime minister. When I once proudly told him I was descended from the "kings of Ireland," he confounded me by saying I must be wrong as, no, he was, and he was not aware that we were related.

Among the students John Main had a reputation for fairness and honesty with firmness. This was strange, as it went with another reputation as a smooth operator. He was openly contemptuous of the corporal punishment still in use and refused to administer it. Although he gave the impression of treating the boys as equals, the boundaries were drawn clearly. As students we knew that some of the teaching staff disapproved of him. My most serious encounters with him just before I left school showed me a clarity and toughness that at the time I felt as sheer stubbornness. One arose after I had gained early entrance to university and so could afford to relax my pursuit of good grades. In particular I saw no point in completing my French "A" level. My appeal for exemption led up to Father John's study, where he welcomed me graciously and invited me to sit down as he lit a cigarette. I noticed with annoyance he did not offer me one. After I explained my case, which he listened to carefully and I thought open-mindedly, his sympathetic listening convinced me that I had convinced him. This hope was shattered as he replied that it seemed to him I was bright enough but needed more self-discipline. Doing French would therefore be just the thing. It didn't particularly matter, he added casually, what you studied provided you learned how to study. I was intrigued by this new approach to school studies but no less furious. Little did either of us realize that many years later what little French I had learned would be of great help to us both in Montreal when I went to help him start a new, very different kind of Benedictine school.

In my last term we learned that Father John was also leaving to go to a monastery in the United States. Having no idea there was even such a thing as monastic politics, I assumed it was a simple decree of providence. As it happened I was going to spend a year working at the United Nations in New York before going to Oxford and was keen for contacts there. I mentioned this to him. He invited me warmly to visit him in Washington and gave me his address.

•

Douglas William Victor Main was born in London in 1926. His paternal grandfather, from a Presbyterian Scots family, had worked on the first transatlantic cable station at the point where it landed from America at Ballinskelligs, County Kerry. There he met and married a local Catholic girl. They settled and raised a family there, and Douglas's father in his turn married a girl from County Meath. There were six children, of whom Douglas was the third, blond, blue-eyed, tall, with a serious and rather delicate look. His father was a colorful independent entrepreneurial personality. Their family fortunes roller-coastered along with stability and continuity provided by their ever-adored mother. It was a devout Catholic family but by no means frightened of the clergy.

When he was about six or seven Douglas was sent for a year to stay with a childless couple, friends or relatives of his parents, in Ballinskelligs. He mentioned it to me only once, and when I later raised it with his family they vaguely connected it with his sensitive constitution and need for fresh air and country food. From his account, however, the idea seemed to be that if he was happy there, and if the couple were too, then maybe he would stay with them permanently. But he was definitely not happy, and he returned within a year to the bosom of his loving family in London. His family's love never failed him, but this early forced experience of detachment marked him too. At an unusually early age he had been forced to learn what separation meant, and also that he could survive it. Throughout his adult life he made many dramatic voluntary decisions to separate from one safe way of life for another less secure and certain. One of his unusual strengths was to make these decisions punctually and decisively in order to allow what was growing in him to expand. This quality of percipient detachment often made him seem unpredictable. It also showed people what unspoken depths he was in touch with in his own destiny.

Not unlike many Catholic boys of his age at that time, Douglas announced when he was twelve that he wanted to be a priest. After studying at a Jesuit school in north London, he went as a chorister scholar to Westminster Cathedral Choir School, where one of his priest teachers oddly detected a "tendency to a Benedictine vocation."

By the time he left school, however, the war was on, and he began to train as a journalist until he was old enough to join the army. Like every episode of his life it provided him with additions to the fund of anecdotes by which he narrated, and some thought created, his life story. He particularly liked to tell how he had been told to review a concert he had not heard and received a letter of praise for what he had written from the conductor. He was a natural storyteller, in the great Irish tradition of the shanachy, or spinner of tales. It was the effect of the story that really mattered more than the literal truth. Frequently this would simply shake up mental complacency with a dash of humor. If daily reality seemed too drab, like many an Irishman he would add color to liven it up.

In 1943 Douglas joined the army and, having already learned Morse code from his father, trained as a wireless operator. For the remainder of the war he served in dangerous missions with the Royal Signals operating behind the retreating German lines, identifying their radio location and passing the intelligence to the Allies. The technology was soon enhanced by the invention of the quartz crystal, which allowed for greater accuracy in detecting radio frequencies. Years later this experience returned to his memory as a way of describing prayer — our way of getting onto the wavelength of the human consciousness of Christ. The mantra he saw as the means of blocking out the distractions of all other mental signals. I was amused recently to hear one of his critics, who had evidently skim-read the passage, accusing him of being "new age" because he seemed to recommend the use of crystals.

His army experience was formative and had an enduring influence. He learned military discipline and a technical skill. Although he was young and innocent and saw a new cruder side to life, he enjoyed the avuncular protection of his elder colleagues in the unit, whose letters home he helped to write for them and who, many years later, remembered him with affection. An explosion in which he was caught caused a recurrent back problem that later confused the diagnosis of his last illness.

After returning to civilian life Douglas quickly joined the Canons Regular, a religious order whose historical luminaries include Erasmus and Thomas à Kempis. It was an austere, drab period of his life — a closed novitiate in Cornwall and studies in Rome under a repressive regime that he came increasingly to find incompatible with his sense of vocation and with the spirit of the gospel. When he began to see that this was not the life for him, his spiritual director, typical of many religious superiors of the time, tried to persuade him this was a temptation of the devil. A less independent spirit could easily have submitted to this manipulation. What helped him to see things clearly was the evident lack of human warmth in the house and its extreme suspicion of the influence of women — two features that his own family life made particularly obnoxious. Such failures of basic humanity he then and later recognized as betrayals of the true meaning of religious life. When he finally left he marked the break with characteristic resoluteness by ceremoniously pushing his habit down the service chute of his sister's flat in London. In later years he expressed gratitude for the study skills he had learned during this period, but on the whole it was not a happy memory.

Douglas went on to Trinity College Dublin to study law. After graduation he joined the British Colonial Service and prepared for his assignment to Malaya by studying Chinese at the School of African and Oriental Studies in London.

In Malaya he continued his Chinese studies and worked in the governor general's private office. He formed many strong personal relationships during his time in Malaya, and he found himself affected by many aspects of Asian culture. Of all the influences of his exposure to the East, however, the most far-reaching was his meeting and relationship with Swami Satyananda. A Tamil Indian born in Malaya in 1909, Swami Satyananda practiced karma yoga, the spirituality of service. As the founder of the Pure Life Society in Kuala Lumpur, he had become well known, in the words of a disciple, as an "apostle of life and pure love and service, a missionary of spiritual socialism."

One auspicious afternoon Douglas Main made an official visit to the swami to thank him for his work. This visit was to become one of the great stories, almost the central myth, of his spiritual journey. Impressed by the achievements, the personality, and the vision of the monk, the younger colonial officer soon found himself in a conversation about prayer. The swami made it a discipline to meditate calmly at 6 a.m. and 6 p.m. each day. When Douglas Main asked if he, as a Christian, could also learn to meditate, the swami laughed and replied that, of course, it would only make him a better Christian. He could teach him provided he was serious about practice — which meant setting aside two periods at the beginning and end of the day, every day. Douglas Main accepted this as well as an invitation to return each week to meditate with the swami and discuss any questions that might arise from his daily practice. At first his questions were typical of all beginners in meditation — how long will this take, when will something happen, am I wasting my time? Sometimes his teacher would discuss the questions, sometimes he would just look at him and smile and help him to see the ego that was pressing the question. Reassurance and encouragement — the meaning of the weekly meeting — was the essential teaching and this was always offered. Each week it resolved again, but ever more deeply, into a simple formula that never lost its wisdom and force for him: "Say your mantra." The heroic simplicity of this practice attracted Main immensely and became one of the most important aspects of meditation he was to emphasize in his own later teaching.

That auspicious afternoon awakened John Main's contemplative journey, bringing consciousness to the deeper movements of his own spirit and greater meaning to the doctrines of his faith. From the outset of his contemplative practice John Main saw meditation as a discipline to follow rather than a technique to employ. Results were to be found in one's life rather than sought in unusual experiences during the actual periods of meditation. A sustained and permanent transformation of the whole person rather than just occasional highs or altered states of consciousness was the goal. In later years he would reject as superficial the Western fascination with techniques to be mastered for spiritual gain. His understanding of prayer was christocentric, and his teaching on meditation explained why. Prayer — and meditation was "pure prayer" — was based indisputably on individual commitment but sustained in love and by spiritual friendship with others. These were among the very first lessons of his practice that he never forgot.

His desire for monastic life was reawakened while he was in Malaya, and this sense of vocation made him refuse an offer of a promotion in Hong Kong. But meanwhile, back in Dublin, his family was in financial difficulties, and so he decided to help out by accepting an offer from his old university to teach International Law at Trinity College. It was another chapter in an already varied life, and a worldly chapter that he enjoyed immensely.

These Dublin years were happy. In fact he had the rare gift of deciding to be happy in almost any circumstances. Above all he loved sharing the daily life of his family and their children. Their independent-mindedness, political and social engagement, like their originality and warmth as a group had already given him the two great strengths of his psychological makeup: self-confidence and the freedom to give and receive love. If it is always easier for the happy to love, then John Main had a good preparation for his deeper exploration of the source of love and true happiness. But in going deeper he had to suffer further detachment.

Dublin life had again forced his monastic thoughts into the background, but experiences of love and death recalled them with urgency. Love came most strongly in the person of a woman he had known many years through family connections, a young English doctor whom he proposed to, was accepted by, and who then shortly after changed her mind and refused him. Years later, he suspected she had, perhaps rightly, feared the intensity of his love and the volatility of his nature. Human love could be an intense passion for him and when unreciprocated caused him corresponding heartbreak. Although a friendship survived the trauma on this occasion the experience of rejection was mortifying. He was not naturally prone to depression; life went on. But he was sorely wounded.

At this moment of great vulnerability and sensitivity death also came to teach him. His eleven-year-old nephew, in whose upbringing he had played an important part since his sister's husband had died, was suffering from what became a fatal brain tumor. On his way home from college one day he stopped at the hospital and found the boy coming to his end. He stayed at his side until the boy's terrible agony was over. In addition to his grief, or because of it, Douglas was confronted with the kind of existential questions of meaning that were not merely intellectual for him but that always drove him to the major decisions of his life. He was overwhelmed by the urgency of finding and responding to life's fundamental meaning and purpose. The question of his own life and vocation rushed upon him and his monastic identity once again asserted itself. Throughout this turbulent period, his daily meditation remained constant. It grounded him in that experience of being, of permanence, to which he was always drawn. Although he was not yet ready to share this aspect of this prayer with others, it gave him the stability and the directional sense that led to his life-changing decision.

Many of his friends and family were astonished. He had seemed so happy! Those who understood him, however, knew he was not becoming a monk either because he was unhappy or scared of life but because, as he himself said, he thirsted for a fuller freedom than he knew he could find in ordinary life. He said he chose an English monastery because he would have lost his faith had he become a monk in Ireland. At his first interview at Ealing he raised eyebrows when he drove up to the monastery in his flashy red M.G. Though the abbot accepted him, the novice master predicted he wouldn't last a month.

He was given the name of John. Then to his surprise and dismay, at a spiritual assessment with his novice master, he came up against the judgment that meditation was a foreign import, alien to the Christian tradition. He was told to give up the meditation that had not only become the foundation of his spiritual life but also led him to become a monk. If he had thought that in giving up the world he had made the great renunciation, the definitive separation, he was learning that of letting-go there is no end. Later he felt no bitterness about the serious spiritual misdirection he had received. Indeed he was able to see it as a work of purification, a detachment from the experience of God that led to a deeper experience of God. When he finally returned to meditation he did so as a result of this interruption "on God's terms rather than my own."

Although the next ten years were spiritually a desert, they were also a time of grace and of a coming home to himself. He had found his real life and had fallen in with the monastic rhythm and style of living as if falling in love. Unlike many who enter religious life or the clerical state he did not put on a religious persona at the time of his clothing with the habit. As in the other chapters of his life he got the most out of these years of formation and study. He did not hide his light under the bushel of false humility. Already matured by life and love, he was free from the usual curse of community life that is overdependent on the approval of others and lack of self-identity. After a traditional novitiate he was sent to study at San Anselmo, the Benedictine university in Rome. It was the church's springtime. Pope John had thrown open the windows of theology and liturgy to new thought. The church was being encouraged to embrace rather than condemn the world. John

Main enjoyed the thrilling atmosphere of *aggiornamento* and
the interaction with monks from other parts of the world.

John Main threw himself enthusiastically into the ferment
of new thought. He formed lasting friendships with European
and American monks and relished Italian life. He made leisurely
trips home during the summer, staying at European monasteries
which his abbot, one of the last gentlemen monks in the English
tradition, considered to be an essential part of monastic training. On his return from Rome he made solemn vows and a year
later was ordained and put to work in the school.

The headmaster of St. Benedict's, Dom Bernard Orchard,
was a broad thinker and imaginative personality with whom
he formed a dynamic partnership to update and develop the
school. The monastery, however, was not unified. Deep ideo-
logical differences and personality clashes simmered behind the
scenes and this eventually brought the headmaster into conflict
with the abbot. John Main could have remained neutral, as he
was advised to do. Had he done so he would have been the
headmaster's obvious successor. But on principle he stood his
ground with Dom Bernard and fell from grace and power with
him. He was criticized for this and suffered for it. John Main
did have the gift of service and loyalty to those whose authority he respected. He lacked the gift for disguising his feelings
when he did not. It is worth knowing of these political circumstances — the monastic equivalent of a marital crisis — only
because they indicate the painful and agitated state of soul by
which he was prepared for the next definitive turning point in
his inner journey.

The departure from office of two of the most dynamic lead-
ers of the community damaged everyone. In their resentment
some were less than generous in deciding the terms of his
exile. Through a friend John Main was offered a teaching and
pastoral position at Oxford University, which he would have
accepted happily, had it been allowed. He was sent instead to

an American monastery in the English Benedictine congregation. St. Anselm's in Washington, D.C., was a rather charmingly eccentric community of anglophiles and scholars with an acclaimed private high school for the intellectually gifted. John Main was sent there, not to work in the school, but to take a doctorate at the Catholic University of America, a convenient and delicately demeaning punishment. His reputation for his involvement in the London crisis preceded him. His first conversation with the abbot opened with a cold discussion of his lodging fees. His first entrance into the monks' common room, like other English congregation houses with its atmosphere of a gentlemen's club, provoked a chilly silence and the raising of newspapers.

It was a very lonely, painful chapter in his life. John Main, however, did not show such feelings readily and with characteristic energy, optimism, and sheer Irish defiance he threw himself into his academic program. At this time I was working in New York and went to visit him in Washington. With no idea of what feelings Father John was carrying inside himself I enjoyed the break, his hospitality and good company. I was pleased by the time he took to show me around town, and I found the monks at St. Anselm's both friendly and intelligent. By then his American brethren were forming their own judgment of him, and before long, to the chagrin of some of his brethren at home, he was invited to become headmaster to sort out a crisis of their own.

•

With this turn of the wheel of fortune his life changed abruptly. His administrative and leadership skills were called upon to rescue the school from a variety of crises. Younger monks working in the school enthusiastically accepted his leadership. As elsewhere he found admirers who felt they could grow in apprenticeship to him. But although he could lead and inspire as

well as empower others he did not want disciples in training.
Even when his reputation as a spiritual teacher had given him
some guru status, he was quick to deflate the role and to bring
those who admired him excessively down to earth with a dose
of his humor and humanity. Some were confused by this. Many
failed to recognize the diamondlike quality of detachment in
his personal relationships. It expressed itself best, however, in
the pleasure he took in seeing others grow into selfhood and
maturity.

Headmastering, even in the difficult circumstances he inherited, seemed a happy occupation for him, and an effortless
one. Before long, he was comfortably established in his authority, lionized by wealthy parents who eagerly welcomed him
into Washington society. All this he enjoyed while remaining
grounded in the rhythm of the monastic life of prayer and
worship. Some at Ealing thought and hoped he would trans-
fer permanently to Washington, but a strong sense of stability
kept him loyal to the place of his first monastic profession. It
also brought him home each summer to visit his aging mother
and the rest of his family.

Over a brief period he had tasted a dark night of the soul and
a new dawn. He had felt the deepest pangs so far in his life of
isolation and rejection and had grown through it. Life was now
again friendly to the needs of the ego. Through all this he had
held the thin golden string that for each person connects the
surface to the depth and that gives a sense of meaning and purpose even to the most mundane as well as the darkest of scenes.
It is the string of faith. The faith he had held on to through all
the cycles of his life would now connect him to that "source of
life" and pure grace that overrules karma.

One day, a young American student fresh from the spiritual
grand tour of the East arrived at the monastery asking for advice on Christian mysticism. Had he known it, a Benedictine
monastery of that type was not the best place to go to find a

living example of the Christian mystical tradition. The abbot referred him on to John Main who, very busy himself, gave him a long book to occupy him. It was *Holy Wisdom,* a seventeenth-century English Benedictine classic by Dom Augustine Baker. It was in fact a strange reading suggestion. Few modern monks get very far in reading it, even if they start, and though Baker is officially admired, he has a mixed reputation among his descendants. His choice of the book suggests something was already changing in John Main, perhaps a sense of the need to renew the meaning of his life by a new exploration of the roots of his tradition. When the young man emerged from a day or two in the library, particularly elated by his discovery of the desert fathers, the fourth-century founders of the Christian monastic movement, John Main found himself drawn back in curiosity and spiritual hunger to these sources of his own tradition of Christian spirituality.

•

It was a revelation, a spiritual watershed as self-defining for him as his meeting with his guru. In fact, these two moments were closely related. John Main was particularly fascinated to read the Conferences of John Cassian, an account of the author's interviews with many of the early desert fathers. In John Cassian's tenth Conference he recognized a treatment of the early practice of the mantra in the Christian tradition. Most Christian readers had assumed that Cassian was speaking abstractly when he described the monks' practice of constantly repeating a "single verse" or *formula,* and spoke of the "renunciation of all the riches of thought and imagination" and fidelity to the "grand poverty" of the prayer of the heart. His *apophatic* approach to prayer — not thinking about God — was seen (at least by his Western commentators) as just another, wordier form of the *cataphatic* approach — thinking about God. In the Eastern church, which regards Cassian as a saint and great master of the inner life, initiation into the tradition of the Jesus Prayer makes his meaning clearer to his readers. John Main had already been initiated. In a shock of revelation he recognized the practice of the mantra itself, the ideal of silence, the stilling of mental activity, and the unself-consciousness of "pure prayer" that he had learned from Swami Satyananda. Even more he saw that Cassian taught this not as a specialized vocation but as essential to the monastic vocation whose primary purpose is to arrive at "unceasing prayer." John Main picked up what he had been told to let drop at the beginning of his novitiate. Now he was reconnected to the path of meditation within an explicitly Christian understanding. He found the signposts illustrated with theological and scriptural references.

In the midst of his duties as headmaster, John Main plunged into the primary sources of his monastic tradition. Things began to fall silently and dramatically in place. He saw the link between Cassian, the Jesus Prayer, and *The Cloud of Unknowing,* a classic mystical text of fourteenth-century England, which also recommend the use of the mantra (without, of course, using that word). He saw that what John of the Cross and many great masters of the Christian tradition did not say about *how* to pray was as important as what they did say about the nature of prayer. He recognized how Abbot John Chapman, a rare contemplative English abbot of the 1930s, had discovered, through fidelity to his own logic of deepening prayer, the simplicity of the single word. He saw what Thomas Merton, the prophet of monastic and church renewal, only recently electrocuted in Bangkok, had bravely been struggling toward.

In John Main the contemplative tradition now had a new manifestation. But for some time it was a hidden, silent emergence. He returned to his own meditation practice, at first twice a day. Before long he began to return to the monastery at lunchtime for a third session. It was a straight run. Illuminating his rapidly deepening inner experience was the complete rereading of the New Testament that he undertook at this time. Passage after passage, most of which had become overfamiliar with years of repetition, shone and shimmered with newfound meaning. The old dictum of Evagrius, Cassian's teacher, that the one who prays is a theologian and a theologian is one who prays, proved itself in John Main. From then on, whenever he read Scripture, people remarked that it sounded as if he had just written it himself. They heard it with a new, illuminating freshness of experience: Jesus' invitation to leave all possessions and follow him in a loss of self, his call to fullness of life, the Resurrection, and St. Paul's declaration of the indwelling of the human consciousness of Christ in the heart of the believer, indeed in every heart. From one of these readings in St. Paul he selected the word that he later gave to beginners as their mantra: *Maranatha*. This is an Aramaic phrase, in the language Jesus spoke, meaning "Come, Lord" (or "the Lord comes"). As one of the earliest of Christian prayers it is a sacred word. It struck him immediately as an ideal mantra (but not the only possible one) with which Christians could begin to clear the mind and which faithful repetition day by day would, as Cassian taught, allow to become rooted in the heart.

About this time I wrote to Father John about some personal grief of my own. I knew nothing of what he had been going through and was not even sure why I was unburdening myself to him. He replied with warmth and perceptiveness and invited me to spend Easter in the monastery. At the end of one of our long talks he told me how to meditate. A better way of putting it would be to say that I realized he had just told me how to meditate. I cannot remember exactly how he put it because the seed was dropped with incredible delicacy, lightly, almost imperceptibly. It took some years to germinate before I meditated regularly, but I had the grace of intuitively welcoming it. Despite my Oxford skepticism and too high evaluation of the intellect, there seemed nothing to argue with about meditation — at least

as John Main presented it. Something so simple, gentle, and absolutely authentic had a self-evident quality: Every morning and
evening, sit down, sit still, close your eyes, repeat your mantra
and keep returning to it when you become distracted. As I recall
he did not pursue my initiation or even ask me if I was doing
it. When I asked to meditate with him he seemed strangely reluctant, as if I was pushing too hard or dramatizing something
very simple. He shared his conviction but did not describe the
experiences he had or that you might have. Yet his very silence
about this aspect of meditation seemed to make his conviction
even more persuasive. His attitude to this came to mind much
later as I read in the gospel how Jesus told his disciples not to
speak publicly about his healing miracles.

Although John Main is seen now as a teacher of meditation
in the Christian tradition and as the founder of a modern school
of spirituality, he always felt that the mantra was caught rather
than taught. He taught from the conviction of experience and
simply offered the teaching. When people wanted to contest
it or to analyze it merely theoretically, he would usually decline. If they would not agree to enter the experience itself in
which the real learning took place, he saw no point in argu-
ing in the abstract. Like turning the other cheek, this attitude
often made opponents even more antagonistic. To some of his
closest friends and family he never spoke about meditation at
all. When those who did learn from him began to form weekly
meditation groups and themselves shared the gift with others
and as a community of meditators came into being, his sisters
joked about his founding a new religion.

Through the profound conversion experience he had undergone, his personality remained functional and normal. The
effects were not yet so obvious. This is not entirely true however. There was a new kind of sober intoxication in him, an
electricity of joy that coursed in and out of him. To some he
seemed an exceptionally gifted and confident personality en-

joying success at the height of his powers. But his next and unexpected act of voluntary detachment indicated the deeper source of his energy. After five years as headmaster in Washington, he resigned and returned home to England.

Immediately he was plunged back into the divisions and tensions of the Ealing community. After an abbatial election, which he lost by one vote, he was made prior, the abbot's second in command. It was not a satisfactory arrangement. His real interest in returning home was not the election but the development of a spiritual center. He had returned to England asking discomfiting questions about the purpose of monasteries in the late twentieth century. In the light of the awakening that followed his resumption of meditation he saw monastic life differently. Were monasteries merely conventional religious institutions providing, as in his congregation, a good education to the offspring of the middle classes? Were they only centers of nostalgia in a directionless modern church?

John Main was now quite clear at least about what his own next step should be. He proposed that the Ealing community give him a house in the monastery grounds that he would renovate and develop as the home of a lay community. The idea at that time was a novel one, but as monasteries are always looking for vocations it seemed to some of the monks a good way of attracting them as well as of keeping John occupied. The new house however was to be the beginning of a far wider challenge to the complacency of monastic institutionalism than anyone suspected. The lay community he formed was a group of six men — women were not allowed into the monastery so could not join the lay community — who committed themselves for half a year to an intensive discipline of daily meditation, manual work in the house and garden, study, and participation in the prayer and community life of the monks. After this spiritual formation — in John Main's developing vision of the usefulness of monasteries — they would normally return to their life in the world.

When I heard of this idea I was intrigued. I decided I would interrupt my new journalistic career and take the six months off and finally learn to meditate properly. I visited John Main one winter evening in the nicely refurbished but ominously empty house on Montpelier Avenue. I told him he seemed like a man sitting alone on top of a great, empty skyscraper he had built. He laughed at this. I picked up his quiet confidence, however, that it would work, that people would come and that its vision would be realized. His confidence about such things did not have the bravado that usually conceals insecurity. You knew he knew what he was doing. His determination had another unusual quality in his capacity to patiently do nothing. Perhaps he didn't know exactly how things would work out, but waiting was a time of preparation or purification. Then when the moment came he would be ready to act decisively. To my surprise he tested my spirits quite strongly when we discussed my joining the community. He made me question my motivation and the prudence of my doing so. It even seemed to me he did not advise it but was leaving it entirely to me to decide. This was characteristic of his way of helping people to discernment. Those who knew he had helped them most also knew he had put the least pressure on them to conform to his views. Often he helped a difficult decision by throwing a striking question into the moral dilemma: Do you want to do the right thing or the convenient thing? he once asked a young woman struggling with an unwanted pregnancy. It was perhaps his own inner freedom that gave him the personal detachment that allowed him to help others without controlling them or diminishing their responsibility for themselves. And it was his loving practice of this detachment — not his preaching about it — that made such compelling demonstration of the fruits of meditation.

•

A mixed group of personalities converged to form the new lay community. Each of us was in some form of critical transition: one emerging from wasted years of drugs, another struggling with a dysfunctional family background, another trying to decide on a career. It was not a therapeutic community. A high degree of discipline was demanded and freedom given. But it *was* a healing community, and all of us were looking for meaning and direction. We were facing the wounds with which life had consecrated us, and Father John as our teacher was helping us to learn from them the way to wholeness.

To do this alone or in a one-to-one relationship would have been difficult enough. To do it in community required an exceptionally strong commitment to one's own humanity and that of others. It needed also stability and confidence in the process. This derived above all from the teacher. It was during this intense period that drew on all his human skills and spiritual knowledge that John Main moved into his truest and greatest role as spiritual teacher or guru. It was the role, finally, in which he was completely himself. Here we were in the 1970s in a middle-class suburb of west London living out a monastic archetype. John Main's method was that of the desert fathers of fourth-century Egypt: teaching by example rather than prescription, affection and attention, personal rootedness, always offering the encouragement to persevere. Discipline was balanced with gentleness, structure with flexibility, predictability with spontaneity, friendship with self-reliance, idealism with pragmatism. He was always available. He was always doing something — fixing something, cleaning, speaking with a visitor — but he was always present, never interfering unless he saw a job being done shoddily, but ever watchful. Friendship formed among us as a community, but he was the hub of the wheel around which everything turned. For us who benefited so much from it in our own growth and self-awareness it was a discovery of the true meaning of an abbot. Television, radio, and smoking were not allowed, but there was an atmosphere of freedom, and in treats and surprises there was fun. For most of us it was a quite new, wonderful experience of fraternity, stabilized by a loving paternity, whose constant, generous concern was to encourage us to grow in self-knowledge and to mature through the honest healing of our wounds. The difficulties seemed short-lived beside the great self-discovery we were making.

Some of the monks appreciated and maybe even envied the spiritual intensity. Others privately mocked what they saw as a personality cult. One remarked to me that the spirit of the lay community was not really Benedictine. There was too much meditation, not enough moderation, and John was too autocratic. I was amazed. Had this monk ever read the Rule of St. Benedict? I wondered. It called itself a "little rule for beginners" and offered a vision of a higher perfection, a deeper wholeness beyond itself. This critical monk so confident in his point of view seemed to idolize a means and turn it into an end. The lay community had its own arrogance, of course, and sense of superiority. But at least, it seemed to me, we were continually being humiliated by confronting our personal failures. To live complacently confusing moderation with mediocrity seemed the worst of all possible options. What in fact was happening in this roller coaster of pride and humility was a clash of vision about the monastic life itself.

We were told that we were an ashram, not a monastery. I realized we indeed were and began to see that this was precisely the point of a monastery — to become an ashram. These criticisms, overt in meetings of the monastic community or whispered outside, challenged John Main to define his own vision of the Benedictine and monastic traditions. We talked long and often about the purpose and form of a modern monastery. The "community of love" seemed to take shape in these conversations. It seemed to us there were two visions of community

in the Benedictine Rule. First there was an ongoing religious institution with hierarchy and structures to ensure continuity. But
there was also a diverse group of disciples drawn to and unified around an inspired teacher. If you analyzed it too deeply
it fell apart. Lived, it was full of contradiction, but if the leadership and the discipleship were right, it could work. To John
Main it was clear that the abbot did not replace Christ as the
teacher but pointed constantly to the real presence and activity
of Christ in the hearts of each member of the community and in
their communal life. I did not fully understand what it meant,
but I began to see that for John Main Christ was a real presence, a living teacher. The intensity of this reality for him gave
him confidence in his own role as teacher, deriving from Christ.
He could say with conviction that in the Christian vision the
first purpose of the visible human teacher is to get out of the
way. Here in this detached house in a London suburb the tradition of the fourth-century Christian desert descended from the
bookshelves and took flesh. John Main was learning what he
had been taught in the silent depths of his meditation. He was
bringing that inner doctrine to consciousness by teaching it, first
in the intimacy of a small group of disciples and soon to a far
wider audience that began to flow into the house. The idea of
the lay community began to transcend itself.

The catalyst for this change was the request from many
people in London to be taught to meditate as Christians. They
could not leave their families or careers to join a monastery
for six months, but did that mean that to learn to meditate
they would have to leave the church? These requests at first
challenged John Main's preconception of the teaching of meditation. Until then he had thought of it as a transmission taking
place within a monastic ambiance. He was quick to see the new
movement of the spirit however. We started in 1975 the first
weekly meditation groups that met at the lay community house.
The first Christian Meditation Center had been born.

These first groups were very diverse, composed of students, people at home, or business people on their way home after work. They would arrive quietly and take a seat in the softly lit sitting room where music was playing. Soon all the chairs were taken so people sat on the floor. Father John would have finished dinner in the monastery and, missing the night prayer in the monastery, would walk across the garden to the meditation house. In his room he would take off his habit, put on a cardigan and prepare for his talk by reading his favorite New English Bible translation of the New Testament. He might jot down some notes on a file index card and come downstairs and take his seat by the stereo. Punctual as always he would stop the music at eight, welcome people, and begin his talk. He went straight to the point and spoke for about twenty minutes. If it was an introductory group — to which people were advised to come for ten consecutive weeks — he would return to basics and always repeat the essential teaching on how to meditate. He emphasized stillness of body, simplicity of approach, and silence of mind. Toward the end of his talk his voice would become quieter and the words slower as the spirit of silence seemed to grow stronger in him. He would play some music, maybe Bach or a Mozart adagio, then remove his shoes and lead the way across the hall to the meditation room. There were red cushions on the floor, chairs around the wall, a candle burning. Those who could not fit into that room stayed where the talk had been given. After a half-hour of complete silence he would return and play music again before inviting questions. He handled questions briefly, often with humor, always considerately; even critical comments received a gentle response. Everyone listened attentively. He was not saying meditation was the only way or that it replaced other forms of prayer. But he believed it was central to the human journey and the religious vision of life. What he said was mind-opening, surprising, refreshing, and delivered with a kind of authority that was new to his audiences.

When this was concluded he would tell any news of interest to what was becoming a community of meditators and then wish all a good night. People left quietly.

Over the next seven years many of these talks to evening meditation groups in London and later in Montreal were recorded. It is as if a tape recorder had been slipped under Meister Eckhart's pulpit. On cassette they continue today to inspire and deepen the inner journey for countless individuals and groups around the world. (I have just returned to my computer to write this from a short car trip during which I played one of his talks.) There is a way of listening to them that never exhausts their value to refresh and renew one's vision of the spiritual dimension of daily living. What is rather extraordinary is that the simple style and short format of his way of teaching seemed to arrive for him ready made. Each talk has a kernel of a single idea often illustrated by a personal experience or story. A relevant Scripture reading gives it depth and universality. The idea is not presented abstractly but in reference to personal inner practice. As the talk draws to an end John Main's voice seems to prepare one for the silence. The talk is more than the words that compose it because it leads the listener up to the threshold of silence. After that it is up to you to do the work, but you have been well prepared and richly motivated. Over the concentrated seven years of his teaching the insights may have deepened — his final talks have a special luminosity — but the message has a rich consistency. The simplicity of his message thus acquires deeper dimensions of meaning but never ceases to be simple. The clarity sharpens without ever blurring the main focus of its vision.

But words, however striking, are also forgettable. What was it that touched and changed people so unforgettably, brought them back weekly, and also sustained a daily practice? The words and ideas delivered with a quiet passion of conviction communicated what words alone cannot. The initiation he gave

to meditation was silent. To experience it one had only to be
open to it, to be ready to be silent and so to admit, first,
that there is something beyond thought. The openness was not
merely intellectual but personal and reciprocal. To many this
was and still is a unique encounter with real spiritual authority in their lives. Meditation was the consistent message and the
medium. But it pointed beyond itself. More than a method of
prayer or a mere technique it is fully understood only as a way
of being, a way of life. It is both the most objective and most
personal wisdom. It is best communicated from an integrated
personality — a holy soul. An authentic, authoritative harmony
of this order existed between John Main's personality and his
teaching. This inner harmony was his gift as a spiritual teacher
also for those who never knew him personally but who have
come to know him personally through his "words of fire."

His communication concerned love. To those who understood that their search for God was a search for love he made
deep, rich sense. To those for whom God and love have been
mentally or emotionally separated or who have given up on
love it was and is much more difficult to understand him. Once
you tune into this frequency and feel the identity of God and
love, his talks open up resounding harmonies. His simple, reiter-
ated teaching opens up a new dimension of spirit to be explored
and to become familiar with. As a teacher, however, he is less
concerned to write a travel book than to give a map and the
encouragement to make the journey for oneself. "In your own
experience," was one of his favorite phrases.

Through his teaching one saw meditation as a way of love.
For him love meant a complete personal union realized as
a turning from self to the other, an abandonment of self-
consciousness consummated in a fullness of being in union with
others and with the ground of being itself. This was gradually
realized through the sustained stillness, silence, and simplicity
of meditation. But it is also the meaning of all personal re-

lationship. Love gives the unifying vision to John Main's life and teaching. It was the certainty and durability he looked for from his childhood. In whatever dimension of experience he looked — psychological, spiritual, and even at the social level — love held the key to right understanding and right action. It was a thrilling perception that gave both tenderness and strength to his personality. It was also completely lacking in the sentimentality — he called it "mawkishness" — with which the ego tries to possess and control love. Joy-filled as this experience was for him he knew it could not be divorced from its tragic implications: love could be born and survive only through the continuous death of the ego.

This ruling perception of love guided the way he helped others into their own vision of God. Both the meditators in the growing community and others came seeking his counsel. His detachment was not a Zen-like aloofness. But having received the gift of his total attention and felt his compassion, you also realized that he had not suspended your freedom. He was not even trying to solve your problems for you. Only those who never trusted him with their souls felt he was telling them the answer. He was doing something deeper and more helpful. What he offered was clarity, perspective, and a refreshing sip from the spring of reality. His most specific recommendation was to undertake a discipline of daily meditation, but this suggestion was simply made rather than imposed. He thought that any discipline that was not freely embraced led to the slavery of fear. What saddened him about much institutionalized monastic life was its prevailing climate of fear and culture of conformity. He did not advocate unrestrained self-indulgence, but there were cases where it might be better to do the wrong thing rather than, out of fear, to repeat the right thing for the wrong reason. Like Cassian, he knew that one learned from facing one's desires and fears rather than repressing or disguising them. Experience, not fear, was the best teacher.

While he was discovering his role in a new kind of spiritual community, the monastery's internal dramas intensified. It was public knowledge that the monks were divided between two distinct kinds of monastic vision represented by John Main and the abbot. St. Benedict had warned precisely about this danger of division between abbot and prior, and despite genuine effort on both sides no resolution seemed likely. John Main's supporters saw him as a charismatic leader who would update the theology and liturgy of their monastic life, bring vitality and innovation, and attract vocations. His opponents suspected his charm and humor and saw him as disturbing the peace, eager for power, articulate in a way the English always find fascinating but frightening.

Neither of these reactions of his brethren would, had they known of them, meant much to the growing number of people who saw in him a rare spiritual teacher. He could have opted out of monastic politics — and therefore out of community — and concentrated only on the easier role in which he found greater recognition. But this would have been so untrue to his character that it was inconceivable. Being himself he was headed for trouble.

In 1976 John Main was invited to lead the community retreat at the Abbey of Gethsemani, the Trappist monastery in Kentucky, where Thomas Merton had lived. Published later as *Christian Meditation: The Gethsemani Talks,* his teaching there was and still remains a seminal introduction to meditation. Although he spoke as a monk to fellow monks, his subject was the universal call to holiness. Monastic spirituality, he said, possessed a pearl of great price to share with the world. Like Merton, he had come to find the spiritual shallowness and superficial busyness of much monastic life increasingly frustrating. He had begun to desire a different, simpler form of life focused on the essential vision of the Christian and the monastic life — a goal that he saw from laypeople's response to meditation was essentially the same for all. He felt that the often bitter hostilities of monastic politics arose from a frustration and loss of the essential purpose of the monastic calling. Without contemplative experience as its fundamental value monasteries could become terribly dysfunctional places, merely centers of human and spiritual mediocrity. Willful mediocrity was perhaps the vice John Main found hardest to tolerate.

The warm-hearted openness of the Trappist monks to what he shared with them touched and inspired him. During the following days that he spent in solitude in Merton's former hermitage his sense of his own future suddenly became sharper. After celebrating what he described to a friend as the "most loving Mass of my life," he knew that he would have to leave Ealing if the life expanding in him was to grow. Soon after, visiting friends in Montreal, he was taken to meet Leonard Crowley, the English-language auxiliary bishop and a man with whose vision and directness he immediately resonated. When he returned to Ealing he carried with him an invitation from Bishop Crowley for the monastery to start a new house in Montreal. This fell resoundingly on deaf ears except for those of the abbot who, like John Main, saw it as the Spirit's solution to the intractable problem of their divisions. Discussions flowed, and finally the community gave its consent. After one further struggle it was even allowed that I (who had now entered the monastery and made simple vows) might go with him.

The English meditators were distraught. Some wrote appealing for an intervention to Basil Hume, the newly appointed archbishop of Westminster and himself a Benedictine monk, one of whose last acts as abbot of Ampleforth had been to invite John Main to lead the monastery's retreat. The wheels, however, were in motion, and on September 28, 1977, we left for Montreal. On the plane I moved back a few rows to watch a film. Halfway through it I thought I saw Father John slumping over in his aisle seat. My first thought was that he was fooling.

When I got to him I saw it was quite serious. Oxygen was ad-
ministered, and he revived. He put it down it to a lung problem
that had caused similar blackouts on planes before. In the excitement of arrival, in teeming rain, and a warm welcome by
Bishop Crowley, this warning of another separation to come
was forgotten.

•

The early days of Montreal perfectly suited John Main's taste
for new challenges and manual work. There was also more time
to meditate. We were largely unknown and so there were fewer
demands. People wondered why two English-speakers were set-
tling in Quebec, while thousands of anglophones were fleeing in
fear of the French separatist movement. John Main relished the
paradox, explaining how the church transcended politics and
that we were bringing a universal language of silence. There
was a lot to do before Christmas when we planned to move
into the old farmhouse that the bishop had acquired for us in
Notre Dame de Grace, a leafy inner suburb, a neighborhood
of young families and friendly dogs. People came to meditate.
Eileen Byrne, an English meditator who had moved to Montreal, had already started a weekly group that we began to
meditate with. We made true friends, found benefactors, picked
up donated furniture for which, in most cases, we were convenient garbage removers. As soon as we moved into the house we
started weekly groups. Our monastic robes stayed in the closet.
The monastic rhythm punctuating the day with regular times of
prayer, Eucharist, and meditation came into being with a new
simplicity that made its purpose crystal clear. This was the integration of ways of prayer that John Main had been longing
for. At Ealing we had meditated in the prayer house and then
walked over to the church to sing the office and to celebrate
Mass. Now the natural connection between chant, Scripture,
and Eucharist fell into a seamless unity. The office was simpler

and shorter but gained meaning as an immediate preparation for meditation. The Eucharist was simpler and longer but, with meditation after the communion, its meaning as the "prayer of Christ" — John Main's central theme about all prayer — shone out.

It was in these early days in Montreal that I came to my first real insight into John Main's Christian faith. Before I had just taken it for granted. What I knew and valued in him were those personal qualities, the fruits of the spirit, which found such deep and infectious human expression. St. Paul calls them the gifts of "love, joy, peace, patience, courtesy, goodness, gentleness, fidelity, and self-control." In no one do these qualities grow in isolation. They arise from the integrated personal wholeness that *is* the spirit, but they are seen and felt separately according to circumstances. At times I was struck by his firm self-control. At others I benefited from his patience. His joyfulness colored his environment and relationships. However as we worked and meditated together day by day on this risky new adventure in Montreal, I came to see what is really meant by a person living the life of Christ. Perceiving it in John Main I knew this did not just mean applying certain ideas or precepts to your life and decision-making. It means knowing yourself in relationship to the person of Christ you are living with and who is therefore also living in you. There is also a conscious affection involved in Christian faith, a love of Jesus not as archetype or ideal but as person, albeit absolute Person. Once I walked past the meditation room and saw Father John kneeling in front of the crucifix in deep prayer. This was so unusual I thought for a moment he had heard me coming and was playing another joke. When he became aware of me I saw that he had simply fallen to his knees because a wave of love had overwhelmed him. Without embarrassment, seeing perhaps that I had learned something at that moment, he shared with me more of what he knew of the love of Jesus.

More often this was expressed silently: in the deep silences
that punctuated his way of saying Mass, in the total absorption
of body and mind that he seemed drawn into when he meditated. To see him meditating and to meditate with him was a
teaching of its own.

This experiment in urban monasticism took off and won
general approval. More and more people came to join our regular times of prayer. The evening groups became milestones in
people's weeks and in their lives. Visitors from overseas were
put up in a nearby convent or in the apartment where some
of the Ealing lay community stayed at the corner of Avenue
de Vendome. A young family brought their children, and a
meditation group for children started on a Saturday morning.
The abbot of Ealing paid a pleasant visit. John Main began to
receive invitations to speak from around the continent.

He was in his element. Starting and making things work were
his delight. The many chores and repairs around the house,
sessions with plumbers and carpenters, getting and arranging
furniture or bargaining with wholesalers absorbed his passion
for detail. Barbecues on summer evenings at which the friends
of the community and guests mingled gave him the pleasure of
being a host and father of a family. Dealing with the personal
crises and needs of this immediate family evoked his compas-
sionate and strong fatherly side. Meeting with businessmen,
benefactors who were impressed by his worldly *savoir faire,*
entertained the secular side of his personality. Nevertheless all
the busy demands of a new community were subordinated to
the regular observance of the prayer times that now included
four periods of meditation in common. Someone gave us an old
chiming clock, which made us all the more punctual. Rather
than being distracted or disrupted by these activities, John Main
appeared to find a deeper place of peace in himself. His personal
harmony — all these things absorbed aspects of his personality — grew stronger and from this inner strength the clear

precise tone of his teaching came ringing more clearly day after day.

His first published books (*The Gethsemani Talks* and *Word into Silence*), a set of tapes, and a quarterly spiritual letter sent to a growing list of meditators around the world, as well as retreats in the United States and Europe, brought him into contact with a widening range of spiritual seekers. His reading was mostly accomplished as usual in the hours before sunrise when he rose in a still sleeping house to meditate alone and study. He deepened his reverence for the eastern tradition, contemporary philosophy, and religious thought in the light of his discoveries about the universality of meditation. In the spring of 1980 he was invited to welcome the Dalai Lama at an interfaith service at the Catholic cathedral. He persuaded the organizers to include a substantial period of meditation to bring the different faith traditions together at depth. The Dalai Lama told him it was the first time he had meditated in a Christian church. The following Sunday the Dalai Lama arrived with his retinue at our small house-monastery to meditate at noontime. He had lunch with the community and then spent an hour alone in conversation with John Main in his room.

Idyllic as this period is now in memory, as we lived it we knew even then it would be short-lived. Almost from the beginning we were searching for a larger house. There were many disappointments and false trails but eventually a miracle dawned. We were offered a large mansion, a Florentine-style villa gardened in the heart of Montreal and filled with beautiful pieces of Renaissance art, many of them from European monasteries. It seemed a typical example of divine humor. Everyone was intoxicated by the magnificence of providence (and the donors). Having won the trust and admiration of the wealthy Protestant donors, John Main was the hero of the hour. But as usual, while enjoying the success he was detached from the excitement. As he walked me round the house for the first time,

he warned me to see beyond it as well. It would not, he said,
be our last step.

•

The monastic mansion on Pine Avenue gave Father John a
whole new array of practical tasks that he took on enthusiastically. But he knew the honeymoon phase of the new community
was over. People were impressed, sometimes overawed, and
some scandalized by the big new house. He saw its value simply
as a platform or springboard to give greater range to the message about meditation as the lost link of Christian spirituality.
Numbers grew. The new meditation rooms and chapel were
much larger and were soon full. But a tension between the function of the meditation center and the needs of the community
that ran it began to develop, which in fact did not reach its cli-
max until several years after his death. But he also saw how the
style of the house was affecting the more intimate quality of the
community as it had developed on Vendome Avenue. Novices
were received, habits were worn, and there was a "cloister
area." After a while we questioned if these developments, while
gratifying in themselves, in fact represented progress in the
monastic vision that had grown out of a meditating community.

He began to work on a new version of the Rule of St. Benedict and to think about the need for solitude. When the Benedictine abbot primate arrived on a visit from Rome, he and John
Main discussed starting a new congregation in the Benedictine Order that would comprise the other independent houses
that, like us (in association with a New York monastery),
were under the primate's personal supervision. But it would
be a congregation of contemplative communities expressing a
more contemporary interpretation of the fifteen-hundred-year-
old Rule. This idea, together with his deepening attraction to a
solitary life out of the city, began to occupy John Main's imagination. We spoke of the big house as a city meditation center

and of a related smaller, more solitary community in the country — where the distinction between monk and layperson need not be so defined. Like many a Celtic (and Benedictine monk) before him, as soon as he had made one home he began to look ahead to the next.

This particular future, however, began to fade with a new concern for his health. In the fall of 1979 he had been diagnosed with colon cancer. The operation was uncomplicated and was called a success. He was encouraged to be optimistic, and this he found easy to do. When I visited him in the hospital the night before the operation, I was not surprised to find him radiantly peaceful and ready to strengthen me. I *was* surprised by the depth of his peace and resignation that seemed to have reached a new, actually blissful intensity. Physically thinner and with a white beard, he had visibly aged. I think even at this point, three years before he died, he had looked into the eyes of death and greeted his mortality. While he was happy to take on the doctors' optimism he knew he had received a warning, and the tick of life's clock sounded louder. He convalesced quickly, however, and then escaped the Canadian winter for the month of January at a monastery in the Bahamas, where he rested, swam, walked, enjoyed an evening glass of rum, and edited the first collection of his newsletters, *Letters from the Heart.* Immediately afterward he resumed a physically demanding round of travel and teaching and the increasingly challenging running of the expanding community.

At home the weekly meditation group and the homily at Mass were his supreme teaching moments. He accepted retreats and conferences from a sense of the responsibility to spread the teaching of meditation in the church. He spoke challengingly, prophetically, about the diminishing of the Christian spiritual life, its faith long eroded by lack of personal experience, and the loss of the authority of Christianity in a world hungry for wisdom. The new pope, John Paul II, had been greeted hopefully by

the world and church, but it soon became clear that he wanted
to draw a sharper line between the church and the world.
His genuine vision and charisma enriched the church's social
teaching but also slowed down ecumenism and the process of
renewal that had begun with the Second Vatican Council. The
line between conservatives and liberals also began to grow divi-
sively. John Main took an active interest in these developments,
but his response was from a contemplative rather than political position. He saw deeper, more long-term signs of hope for
Christianity. He found them especially in the proliferation of
small meditation groups around the world already meeting in
homes, churches, schools, prisons, offices, and hospitals. The
personal atmosphere of these groups illustrated the new form of
Christian community that emerges from shared contemplative
experience and discipline. New kinds of Christian teachers and
witnesses were maturing in the silence of these weekly groups
and their own daily practice. These intuitions inspired his hope
for the future and drew out some of the deepest of his insights
he wanted to share.

These insights were not part of a systematic theological dis-
course. They were living theology, springing from experience,
enriched and shaped by tradition. They expressed themselves
in some of the themes that form the following anthology: the
simplicity of meditation, the transcendence of egotism and self-
consciousness, the definitive effect on human nature of the life,
death, and resurrection of Jesus, the prayer of Jesus as the tem-
plate of all human experience of God, the divine primacy of love
in all things human, the need for discipline and for knowing
one's full potential, and the rediscovery of gospel joy.

•

When his cancer returned at the beginning of 1982 his sense
increased of the urgency of the message of meditation for a
troubled world. During the worst of the Cold War he had

wondered if the nuclear disaster everyone feared might be triggered by a slip-up in a computer program. Looking now at the triumph of capitalism he saw another more insidious danger — humanity's intoxication with affluence, technology, and the illusion generated by virtual reality. He spoke more frequently about the social relevance of meditation as well as its mystical significance. He spoke of the need to develop a community of men and women of spiritual maturity who could teach meditation. Like his friend Bede Griffiths, the English Benedictine who had arrived at many of the same insights from his ashram in India, John Main never lost faith in the importance of monasteries. But he found more hope for the future in the phenomenon of a contemplative laity, the meditation groups and the worldwide Benedictine oblate community of meditators who interpreted the Rule in the light of their lives in the world.

Soon the big new house became his place of illness rather than, at least for him, the springboard to another chapter in the spiritual adventure he had imagined. The chemotherapy was not working. In the final months he suffered greatly from the cancer as it spread to his lungs and then to the spine. He was increasingly in a wheelchair, as when he attended the surprise party prepared by the oblates on the fifth anniversary of our arrival in Montreal. The doctors were concerned about the danger of the spine snapping and the resultant paralysis. Radium treatment in late November of 1982 helped reduce the pain, but each day had landmarks that were no longer reachable: something he did today he would not be able to do the next. But the doctors could give no better prognosis than two days or two years. It was unpredictable yet hopeless. He did not want to destabilize the anxious community further so did not talk much about the illness.

Living with him was always to live at a greater than normal intensity. The final months even more so. Each day had a divine spark, and the most mundane of things glowed with signifi-

cance. Negative and positive emotion might swing one way or
another, but there was always a grounding sense of purpose and
direction. His particular kind of holiness radiated from a silent,
conscious connection with the ground of his being. He called
on this connection directly even more often during the day as
he dealt with the approach of death. His way of being illustrated two essential aspects of his teaching that this anthology
portrays: continuous prayer, the ideal that had led him back to
meditation, and detachment from all that is transitory. Even his
pain threshold benefited from this deep mindfulness and detachment. His personal harmony and wholeness had always created
a spiritual climate that affected those around him. His by now
virtually continuous practice of detachment and immersion in
the state of prayer intensified it.

He was increasingly silent yet did not appear withdrawn.
His silence made him more present. It intensified the quality of
his love and kept it free from sentimentality. At times a little
"mawkishness," as he called it, might have been welcomed by
those caring for him and struggling with their feelings. But the
reward of truthfulness was greater in the end. When his friend
Rosie Lovet, who came for some weeks to help care for him,
was leaving, both knowing that they would not see each other
again, he merely said with a smile "So you are leaving today!"
If there had been only this detachment and control of emotion, then his dying would still have been true to his teaching —
but not exceptionally significant. There was another lesson life
had taught him, which had formed his central teaching and
which his manner of dying confirmed: the energy of love is the
supreme reality. In his presence during these last days it was
love that you felt emanating from him and penetrating you —
an intensely directed, personal yet transcendent communication.
Personal and more than personal. He became increasingly silent
in that love as if he was being absorbed by it or becoming it.
One saw the full, terrible beauty of the meaning of simplicity.

When I asked him what I should do, as I was being left holding the baby, he replied, "You will do what you will have to do." This disappointed me at the time but also empowered me. Immediately he added, in a matter-of-fact tone of voice, that of course he would continue to be present. There was faith in these words. He convinced me effortlessly that he absolutely knew what he had faith in.

In October he gave a talk at the International Palliative Care Congress in Montreal organized by his friend and physician Balfour Mount. Sitting as he spoke because of the pain in his spine, he spoke there of death as a stage of life, part of an inner journey in which meditation has a peculiar power to intensify life. To meditate, he said, is to prepare for one's death and thus to live life more meaningfully because it helps us die the small daily deaths of the ego. He gave his last talk to a meditation group meeting at the monastery two weeks before he died at 8:45 on the morning of December 30, 1982, with those he loved and who loved him at his side.

Some weeks before he died he had two intense dreams that he interpreted as his psyche preparing him for death. In the first he was talking to his elder brother outside his room in the monastery. As he walked across the landing he heard someone running up the stairs. He thought it was his brother, but as the figure rushed past him at the top of the staircase he saw with a shock that it was himself. In the other dream he was standing on the platform of a small English village station waiting for a train. A modern train pulled in, so new that the only way in was through the windows. He started to climb in but got stuck in the window and the train started off. People began to shout instructions, but he could not hear them and no one pulled the communication cord. Dom Rupert, his old abbot who had received him into the monastery, was in the train.

These dreams were a psychic anticipation of death. Perhaps they also helped him recapitulate a lifetime of self-discovery and of many departures. Selfhood was found in the meeting with otherness, ultimately the great Other we call God. Letting go of what one had gained ensured progress. Until the final destination one's entry into reality would be incomplete. Monastic life — like every kind of life that is lived fully — was for him a journey, not an end in itself, a sequence of departures. But the golden string that connected the chapters and that led home was always love. One had only not to let go of that, as one should not let go of the mantra.

When he had passed the biological and psychic barriers of fear, he knew the tide of death could not be turned. Then he embraced the process of dying with the same determination and absolute commitment with which he had thrown himself into all the transitions of his life. This was the final separation that he knew all the others had prepared him for. It was inexplicably early in the chronology of life — at fifty-six — but he looked away from that sadness into the rightness, the necessity that he believed it must have in a deeper scheme of events. His wholeheartedness in accepting death was typical of the way he lived. Total commitment and detachment is a rare achievement in any life. It gave him much more to give. Up to and through his death he shared the power to make life more fully alive.

From his serious-minded youth, always somewhat veiled by his vivacity, life had no satisfying meaning except as a pilgrimage — toward God, into God, to *be* God. Christ for him was the journey in the fully human. Experience. Adventure. Discovery. These were the terms he used to describe the human journey. Meditation for him is the narrow little path that leads to life. It is a door into the silence of God, a way within the greater Way. In that silence, he said, "God answers all questions and all the yearnings of our heart with a simple answer of love. His love is our hope."

When I had first turned to him for wisdom and guidance, I discovered to my surprise that the real power behind his strength and authority was the courage to love. He never doubted that the "meaning of life is the mystery of love." Everything he discovered and taught about what it means to be human confirmed the accuracy of this simple but absolute truth.

A Note on Language

John Main taught at a time when social sensitivity to inclusive language was just dawning. If at times his language does not reflect this, it does not indicate that he was not entirely conscious of the equality of all human beings as well as the particular gifts associated with men and women.

1

Prologue

✛

John Main's teaching on meditation expresses his deepest and most intimate experience of love, of God, of reality. Yet he does not seem usually to speak about himself. Unlike other more autobiographical teachers, he does not lay out his feelings or day-to-day experiences. This is partly due to his temperament. Another reason is that his purpose in teaching at all was not to speak about himself but to encourage others to undertake the contemplative journey he personally knew led to integration and inner peace. He wanted to get people to meditate or at least to know that they could meditate if they wanted to.

For these reasons this section is quite short. The following passage is from the first of the historic talks he gave at the Abbey of Gethsemani in 1976. In this account of his discovery of meditation the deepest point John Main makes is significant both for his personality and his teaching. This point is not the importance of a teacher, nor the radical simplicity of meditation, nor even the value of meditation itself, although these are all important elements of his message. It was the experience of being told to give up meditation — at a time when he least expected it, just as he was becoming a monk, and just when it had become the most important part of his existence — that he learned the deepest meaning of meditation. As he later under-

stood it, he was being taught the way of detachment, even from
that which was most sacred to him. He also learned firsthand
the typical aversion of the church to the contemplative experi-
ence and the suspicion that it was somehow foreign. This time
in the wilderness gave greater significance to John Main's redis-
covery of the Christian roots of contemplation and his recovery
of this way for modern men and women.

I was first introduced to meditation long before I became a
monk, when I was serving in the British Colonial Service in
Malaya. My teacher was an Indian swami who had a temple
just outside Kuala Lumpur. When I first met him on some
official business or other, I was deeply impressed by his peacefulness and calm wisdom. I was pleased to see that he seemed
willing to talk on a personal level once our business was concluded and we fell into conversation. He then asked me if I
meditated. I told him I tried to and, at his bidding, described
briefly what we have come to know as the Ignatian method of
meditation. He was silent for a short time and then gently remarked that his own tradition of meditation was quite different.
For the swami, the aim of meditation was the coming to awareness of the Spirit of the universe who dwells in our hearts, and
he recited these verses from the Upanishads: "He contains all
things, all works and desires and all perfumes and tastes. And
he enfolds the whole universe and in silence is loving to all. This
is the Spirit that is in my heart. This is Brahman."

The swami read this passage with such devotion and such
meaning that I asked him if he would accept me as a pupil to
teach me how to meditate in this way. He replied: "Meditation
is very simple . . . all you have to do is meditate. If you would
like to learn I will try to teach you. What I suggest is this . . . that
you come out and meditate with me once a week. Before we
meditate I will tell you a few things, but the important thing is
that we meditate together."

I began to visit the holy man regularly, and this is what he told me on my first visit. He said: "To meditate you must become silent. You must be still. And you must concentrate. In our tradition we know one way in which you can arrive at that stillness, that concentration. We use a word that we call a mantra. To meditate, what you must do is to choose this word and then repeat it, faithfully, lovingly, and continually. That is all there is to meditation. I really have nothing else to tell you. And now we will meditate."

And so every week for about eighteen months, I went out to this holy man of God, sat down beside him, and meditated with him for half an hour. He told me that provided I was serious in my quest it was absolutely necessary to meditate twice a day for half an hour and to meditate twice a day, every day. He said: "Meditating only when you come out to see me will be a frivolity. Meditating once a day will be a frivolity. If you are serious and if you want to root this mantra in your heart, then this is the minimum undertaking...that you meditate first thing in the morning for half an hour and sometime in the evening for half an hour. And during the time of your meditation there must be in your mind no thoughts, no words, no imaginings. The sole sound will be the sound of your mantra, your word. The mantra (he continued) is like a harmonic. And as we sound this harmonic within ourselves we begin to build up a resonance. That resonance then leads us forward to our own wholeness.... We begin to experience the deep unity we all possess in our being. And then the harmonic begins to build up a resonance between you and all creatures and all creation and a unity between you and your Creator."

I would often ask the swami: "How long will this take? How long will it take me to achieve enlightenment?" But the swami would either ignore my crassness or else would reply with the words that really sum up his teaching and wisdom: "Say your mantra." In all those eighteen months this was the essential core of everything he had to say: "Say your mantra."

On my return to Europe to teach Law at Trinity College, Dublin, years before the advent of the Beatles and the discovery of T.M. [Transcendental Meditation], I found no one who really knew about meditation, as I now understood it. I first tried to raise the subject with priest-friends, but to my surprise my inquiries were mostly received with great suspicion and sometimes even hostility.

About this time, 1958, a nephew of mine, one of my sister's children, became seriously ill and died. The death of this child had an enormous effect on me and brought me face to face with the question of life and death and the whole purpose of existence. As I reviewed my life at this time I was forcibly struck by the fact that the most important thing in my entire existence was my daily meditation. I decided, therefore, to structure my life on my meditation and sought to do so by becoming a monk.

On becoming a monk, however, I was given another method of meditation, which I accepted in obedience in my new status as a Benedictine novice. This new method was the so-called "prayer of acts" — that is, a half hour spent in acts of adoration, contrition, thanksgiving, and supplication, a half hour, that is to say, of prayer that was largely words addressed to God in the heart and thoughts about God in the mind.

In retrospect I regard this period of my life as one of great grace. Unwittingly my novice master had set out to teach me detachment at the very center of my life. I learned to become detached from the practice that was most sacred to me and on which I was seeking to build my life.

Instead I learned to build my life on God himself. The next few years were bleak years in terms of spiritual development, but I always went back to the obedience which was the foundation of my life as a monk. I think too that somewhere deep inside of me there was a faith that God would not leave me forever wandering in the wilderness and would call me back on to the path. What was important was that I should come back on his terms and not on my own.

Finally, there came a stage in this retrogression when everything seemed set for an eternal postponement of any urgent action in getting back to a more vital life of prayer. I became headmaster of St. Anselm's School in Washington, D.C., and was plunged into the busiest time I have ever had in monastic life. The urgent issues were the raising of money for a new science wing, college placement, examination ratings. In the midst of all this, however, a young man came to the monastery asking to be taught something about Christian mysticism. He had spent time with a Hindu teacher but was now looking for the Christian standpoint. So with some malice aforethought I gave him Baker's *Holy Wisdom* as his first book of study, thinking that this would keep him quietly occupied for several weeks, unraveling its loping, Drydenesque sentences. To my amazement, however, he reacted with real and immediate enthusiasm, to such a degree that I felt I had to read it again myself. We began to read it together and very soon afterward we also began to meditate together.

Baker's frequent reminder of the emphatic insistence St. Benedict lays upon Cassian's Conferences sent me seriously to them for the first time. It was with very wonderful astonishment that I read, in his Tenth Conference, of the practice of using a single short phrase to achieve the stillness necessary for prayer.

> The mind thus casts out and represses the rich and ample matter of all thoughts and restricts itself to the poverty of a single verse.

In reading these words in Cassian Chapter X of the same Conferences on the method of continuous prayer, I arrived home once more and returned to the practice of the mantra.

—CM 13–18

Perhaps the greatest problem affecting our society is that so many people feel that they are not fully alive. They suffer the sense that they are not fully authentic as human beings. A major reason for this is that there are so many living their life second-hand without a real openness to the uniqueness of the gift given to them: their own life.

So many lives are lived by responding to other people's goals for us, society's goals for us, the advertising industry's goals for us. Christian revelation says that each of us is summoned to respond directly to the fullness of our own life in the mystery of God. How then are we to break out of the enclosed circle of inauthenticity and its consequent lifelessness? There is only one way and it is the basic message of the New Testament: to be fully open to the gift of eternal life.

The gift of life to each person is itself an invitation to development — an invitation we deny or refuse at our peril. No matter what fears or desires hinder our acceptance there is no ultimate reason why we should not be open to the "life found in the Son" to be encountered in the deep center of our being.

— WMF 38

2

Holy Mystery

While he may have first experienced the practice of silent prayer in the East, there is no doubt that John Main's teaching was thoroughly rooted in his ever deepening Christian faith and his profound grasp of the Gospel of Jesus. Indeed, John Main had an almost Pentecostal enthusiasm for the message of Christianity. His rereading of the New Testament in the light of meditation regenerated his passion for God and his excitement about the Christian contribution to this perennial mystery.

But we can know God only if we know ourselves. Taking the human as the starting point for understanding God frees the concept of God from the dogmatic and psychological baggage it has acquired through religious history. But it also underscores the vital significance of our primary means of self-knowledge, our prayer. For John Main knowledge of God is an experience undergone by the whole person, not merely an achievement of thought. It unleashes forces of change and radical conversion. Privately, half-humorously, John Main would sometimes warn people about playing with the fire that is God if they were not prepared for the consequences. "It is a terrible thing to fall into the hands of the living God," he would quote with a twinkle in his eye.

Knowing God is both a disturbingly personal and universal experience, thanks to Jesus, who ushers in a new age in the human knowledge of God. The old anthropomorphism is made redundant by the Incarnation. Through Jesus, we are given access to a deeper contemplative consciousness that relativizes ritual and dogma and reconstitutes religion. God is revealed as love, the source of compassion and forgiveness, universal and unifying experiences within the deep structure of human existence. As we experience ourselves not merely as acceptable to God, as theology tells us, but as accepted by God, as the heart experiences it, God is not a distant source or destination, but the central reality of our lives.

Meditation is the experiential discipline that leads to this new liberty of God-awareness. Start with God as nothing — abandoning all images and ideas — and you will arrive at God as all. It is not an easy progression, but John Main encourages the new meditator to see it as like falling in love. Knowing God is not understanding a platonic idea but a losing of one's self in the other. It is to enter the Trinitarian explosion of creativity, in which dualism is dissolved by the fire of love.

In this perspective Jesus, for John Main, is the trailblazer whose presence is fully activated on both the human and divine frequencies. He has a terrestrial and a cosmic life, and he shares his presence to and with God with all his fellow human beings. He is the "completely free man," the "fully realized man," the "man wholly open to God," as well as the "center where all lines converge."

John Main stressed the importance of the humanity of Jesus of Nazareth, who awakened to himself within the mortal limitations we all know. But in his awakening he heard himself spoken as the Word. He knew himself as the Son receiving and reciprocating the Father's love. His human self-knowledge thus plunged him into divinity. And so his self-discovery has more than an individual significance. It is the "single and all-inclusive awakening" of human consciousness to its source in God. Jesus can be said, then, to "share" his experience with us and to invite each of us to enter his experience of the Father as our experience. In so doing he explains the human vocation to share in the being of God. So it is the human consciousness of Jesus that inserts us into the center of Being itself and connects us with the flow of the Trinitarian love that is the simple structure of reality. John Main's approach to the uniqueness of Jesus thus goes a long way to dispel the trap of exclusivism into which he saw Christians too easily fall.

Jesus is therefore our goal. But he is not our terminal point. When we have arrived at union with him, he then becomes our departure point to the Father, the source of Being and the Other to whom Jesus constantly refers in the gospels. Christian experience cannot therefore be adequately expressed by theology or church affiliation but only by the human experience of Jesus himself. Freed from fear and desire and tasting harmony with ourselves and others through him, the Christian begins to see the universal influence of the Risen Jesus. This is the mystery of unity that makes us truly human and humane. Jesus is the "universal Christ" who refreshes our vision of reality at every level, in every context.

Meditation continuously refines the identity of a Christian. This identity is no longer defined as belonging to a cult but as being a personal disciple in community. The Resurrection, which occupies the inspirational center of John Main's faith, is no longer a news story we hear but feel no part of. It is an experience of seeing and recognizing the risen Jesus, first of all in the interior dimension, but then in an outwardly expanding range of vision. He is seen with an eye of faith that has foregone its attempt to see itself. As ever, to see, to pay attention, demands stillness.

GOD

Finding Our Roots

What we each have to discover for ourselves is that God is the root from which we are sprung. He is the ground of our being. The most elementary sanity requires that we live out of this rootedness. Living our lives rooted in Christ, knowing ourselves rooted in him, as a daily experience in our daily return to meditation, means that we enter into a radical stability that is impervious to change, to passing, ephemeral contingency. In the silence of our meditation, we gain an experience of ourselves as beyond contingency. We know that we are and that we are in God and that in him we discover our own essential identity and unique meaning. The wonder of Christian prayer is that what we discover is that we have meaning for God. The astonishingly, barely believable thing about Christian revelation is that our meaning is not less than to bring perfection to God. That is, to be so in harmony with him that we reflect back to him all the brilliance of his own glory, all the fullness of his own self-communication.

St. Paul tells us that "in him you have been brought to completion." The Christian mystery summons each of us to enter into the divine milieu and to take our own appointed place within it. The fullness of the Godhead dwells in Christ and Christ dwells in us. In his indwelling we find our own completion. To be complete as human beings we must live this mystery not just intellectually, not just emotionally but with our full being. What the New Testament cries out to us is that the fullness of being we are summoned to, dwells within our being as it is now and is realized when our being and the being of God come into full resonant harmony. Meditation invites us to enter the resonant harmony of God.

Beyond a certain point language always fails us. But we have to try to use language to direct our attention toward the mystery and its depth. The mantra takes up where language fails. It is like God's harmonic. By rooting it in our heart, every corner of our heart, every fiber of our being is open to him and every ounce of his power is channeled into us. That is why we must learn to say the mantra faithfully, continually, and in ever deepening poverty. Sainthood, wisdom, are simply names for reality. God is Real. We discover by that daily fidelity in our meditation that godliness is full sanity. Full sanity flowing from the full power of God's love. Each of us is summoned to discover that this godliness flows freely in the depths of our own heart.

—MC 37–38

The mystery of our relationship with God is one that embraces such a vast canvas that only by developing our capacity for awe-filled and reverential silence will we ever be able to appreciate even a fraction of its wonder. We know that God is intimately with us and we know also that he is infinitely beyond us. It is only through deep and liberating silence that we can reconcile the polarities of this mysterious paradox. And the liberation that we experience in silent prayer is precisely liberation from the inevitably distorting effects of language when we begin to experience God's intimate and transcendent dominion within us.   —WS 7

We know then that we share in the nature of God, that we are called even deeper into the joyous depths of his own self-communion, and this is no peripheral purpose of the Christian life. In fact, if it is Christian and if it is alive, our life must place this at the very center of all we do and aim to do. "Our whole business in this life," said St. Augustine, "is to restore to health the eye of the heart whereby God may be seen." This eye is our spirit. Our first task, in the realization of our own vocation and in the expansion of the kingdom among our contemporaries, is to find our own spirit, because this is our lifeline with the Spirit

of God. In doing so, we come to realize that we participate in
the divine progression and that we share the dynamic essence of
God's still point: harmony, light, joy, and love.   — WS 28

A Relationship of Love

Every personal loving relationship has its source in the movement from lover to beloved, though it has its consummation in
a wholly simple communion. If the Christian mystery depended
upon the strength of our desire for God for its authenticity, it
would be no more than a nostalgia for the numinous. But the
actuality of our faith derives from the initiative that God has
taken. "The love I speak of," wrote St. John, "is not our love
for God, but the love He showed to us in sending his Son."
The natural lethargy and self-evasiveness of man, his reluctance
to allow himself to be loved, are, like the locked doors, no im-
pediments to the Holy Spirit. The Spirit has been sent into the
human heart, and it lives out the divine mystery there for as
long as God sustains man in being. In the heart of the utterly
evil person, were there such a person, the Holy Spirit would
still be crying: "Abba, Father," without ceasing.   — WS 37

The spiritual man or woman is one who is "in love" — in
love within themselves beyond dividedness, and loving toward
all people beyond division. And most miraculously we are in
love with God beyond all alienation, in Jesus. St. Paul says "for
through him we both alike have access to the Father in the one
Spirit." If you live it at the level of words Christianity is unbelievable. We couldn't believe that it is our destiny to have
such perfect access to the Father and the Spirit. It is beyond
what the human mind could think of or comprehend. It is only
in the experience of prayer that the truth of the Christian revelation engulfs us. That is the invitation of Christian prayer, to
lose ourselves and to be absorbed in God.   — MC 25

The only analogy I know of that does justice to this way of wisdom and vision is the analogy of falling in love. When we have fallen in love — and are still falling, still letting go of ourselves — the beloved changes before our eyes, while remaining the same in all appearances to others not caught up in this vortex of love. Loving the other deeply and unreservedly, we see them in a new light, which burns away (makes us forget) our own self-important isolation and allows the smallest gesture of theirs to reveal in us what no one else can recognize. That is why falling in love is so important for us because it sweeps us out of ourselves and beyond the limitations of fear and pride into the reality of the other. Until we can lose ourselves and find ourselves again in the other I don't believe any of us can ever know what liberty really is.

Profound meditation is of the same order. Our silence, stillness, and our fidelity to the simplicity of the mantra serves to lead us away from our isolated self-centered view of life. We are "realized" or "fulfilled" in meditation only because we have ceased to seek or desire realization or fulfillment. We learn to be joyful only because we have learned not to possess, not to want to possess. The ordinary discipline of our daily meditation increasingly shifts our center of consciousness from ourselves into the limitless Mystery of God's love. But first a certain effort is needed to root the discipline in our being rather than just into the routine of our day. We need to have it rooted as an interior as well as an external discipline, so that we can carry it with us through the inevitable changing circumstances of life. Even monasteries change their timetables! When the rhythm of the twice-daily meditation becomes part of the fabric of our being, entirely natural and so always renewed and renewing, then our life is being transformed from the center outward. Then we are learning to see even the appearances of our ordinary life, work, and relationships with the vision of love. The Christian is called to see all reality with the eyes of Christ.

Because we are so used to remaining at the superficial levels of life rather than penetrating beyond appearances, it can seem unbelievable to us that the way to real vision is the transcendence of all images. It seems to us, on the surface, that without images there is no vision, just as without thought there is no consciousness. What takes us beyond this shallowness of unbelief? First perhaps the frustration of shallowness itself, the frustration of finding that year after year we are penetrating no further into the real experience of life, into the real meaning of our own life. St. Paul wrote, "Your world was a world without hope." This is the dilemma of the contemporary world. But what ultimately makes depth of vision possible is faith: the leap into the unknown, the commitment to Reality we cannot see. "What is Faith?" the letter to the Hebrews asked. "Faith gives substance to our hopes, and makes us certain of realities we do not see."

The influence of the scientific method on our entire way of responding to life has persuaded us not to believe in, not to commit ourselves to, anything until we can see the proof of it. The method works well enough for the verification of scientific theory, but it does not work in the dimension of reality that lies beyond appearances. There we must commit ourselves before we see God, because without that commitment there is no purity of heart, no undivided consciousness, and only the pure of heart can see God.   —PC 92–93

JESUS

Entering the Life of God

The reality Jesus has uncovered for us is the new age of Presence. It demands a correspondingly new understanding of how we share in the Trinitarian mystery. Because of the new Christic consciousness, we can understand in a way that is disturbingly personal and universal, that we do not so much exist in relation to God as subsist within God — he is the ground of our being. We are called to know and to know fully, not just notionally, that nothing can be outside the ground of all Being that God is. And so, in the light of Christ, prayer is not talking-to but being-with.

If our knowledge of God stops short at fear of his power over all being, we can see him only as a threat to our being, our conscious survival. So our prayer comes to be a way of pleasing or placating him, and in petitioning him we hope to "turn his anger from us." But all the time the fear has us in the grip or paralysis.

This is God as Creator. But Jesus opens up God to us as Abba, Father. And, in this most personal yet universal of revelations, our dependence upon God is changed from being a source of terror into a source of infinite joy and wonder. We are because God is. God is our being and so our being is good, as he is. We have nothing to fear of such goodness because of the perfect love that is his goodness; the Trinity's explosive creativity burns away all fear. And so the ground of man's most haunting fear — of isolation, fear, and loneliness, that the world is itself only a terrible mistake, an absurd mis-rendering image of reality — is dissolved by the sheer power of God's love.

Prayer, in the Christian vision of reality, is the way we experience that the basic condition of man is not separateness but communion, being-with. This indeed is the Christic-consciousness of love, both commanding and empowering us to be-with everyone out of the harmony of our own basic experience of communion. "Love one another as I have loved you." In giving us his whole self Jesus authenticates this teaching with an absolute and final authority. In the light of this teaching, of this self-giving, and of the consciousness that is communicated we can no longer seriously think of ourselves as summoned to

"surrender" to God. In any surrender we retain the human fail-
ure to dissolve the illusion of dualism. There remains an *I* to
surrender, a *Thou* to be surrendered to. And in the light of the
reality of God it matters little whether such dualism is retained
due to fear or false piety. The result in either case is a kind of
spiritual schizophrenia. We cannot surrender to the one with
whom we are already united. But we can awaken to and realize
our empathy. In the Christic consciousness, and most urgently
for modern people trying to come to terms with this new being,
our relationship with the divine has to be understood in terms
of empathy.   —PC 55–58

The early church was utterly clear that our call is to enter into
the very life of God. No other objective compares with this in
priority. The early Christians also knew that the way we come
to this is through the human consciousness of Jesus, which is to
be found in the deep center of our being. Meditation is simply
the pilgrimage to the heart where we find the Spirit of Jesus
worshiping the Father in love. Jesus is filled with the love for
the Father that is the Father's love for him and that is the Spirit.
Christian meditation is simply to be open to that love which is
the Spirit.   —WMF 32–33

The extraordinary dynamism of the whole of St. Paul's writing is that the marvel, the splendor, the unimaginable reality of
the condition we are in here and now is so overwhelming that
we can hardly keep our concentration steady. We have been allowed to enter the sphere of God's grace where we now stand.
Jesus has blazed the trail for us and through his own experience
has incorporated us in his present state, which is his glorious
communion with the Father in his risen life, a life that now pervades the whole of creation. We stand in the sphere of God's
grace because we are where he is and he is where we are. We
are in him and his Spirit is in us.   —WS 75

What is the basis of the Christian mystery? It is surely that the beyond is in our midst, that absolute reality is here and now. The Christian faith teaches us that by being open to the mystery of this reality we are taken out of ourselves, beyond ourselves, into the absolute mystery which is God. God is how we transcend self. We transcend all limitations by simple openness to the All which is now. The great awakening to the mystery is the kingdom of heaven and the kingdom of heaven is now. It is established by Jesus and proclaimed by his own words, "The Kingdom of God is upon you. Repent and believe in the Gospel." To repent means simply to turn in the direction of God. Repenting is turning not so much away from ourselves (for that keeps us still tied to our own center) but beyond ourselves. This means not rejecting ourselves but finding our marvelous potential as we come into full harmony with God. This awareness of potential is the positive basis of Christianity, and so, for a Christian, the central concern is not self, nor is it sin. The central reality is God and love and, as far as we are concerned, growth in God's love. Growth consists both in our openness to his love for us and in the response we make by returning that love.

"Repent and believe in the Gospel." Believing the gospel simply means being committed to openness to our potential. Each of us possesses unknown potential in the extraordinary plan of personal salvation, and this is what Jesus discloses to each of us in the stillness of our heart as we undertake the journey of silence and of absolute commitment to silence and pure openness every morning and every evening. What he reveals is that we are created for love, for freedom, for transcendent meaning, for fulfillment; and we realize it all by entering the mystery of the kingdom that is upon us. That mystery is now unfolded by the generous gift of Christ.

The kingdom is established. Faith and obedience teach us to realize it. Remember the practicalities of the work of realiza-

tion. Learn to be silent and to love silence. When we meditate
we don't look for messages or signs or phenomena. Each of
us must learn to be humble, patient, and faithful. Discipline
teaches us to be still, and by stillness we learn to empty our
heart of everything that is not God, for he requires all the room
that our heart has to offer. This emptiness is the purity of heart
we develop by saying the mantra with absolute fidelity. The
mystery is absolute truth, absolute love, and so too our response
must be absolute. We respond absolutely by becoming simple.

—HC 106–7

Word and Silence

"It is better to be silent and real than to talk and be unreal," wrote St. Ignatius of Antioch in the first century, and our
contemporary situation must surely bear this out. Authority,
conviction, personal verification, which are the indispensable
qualities of the Christian witness, are not to be found in books,
in discussions, or on cassettes, but rather in an encounter with
ourselves in the silence of our own spirit.

If modern people have lost their experience of spirit, pneuma,
or essence, in which their own irreducible and absolute being
consists, it is because they have lost their experience of and
capacity for silence. There are few statements about spiritual
reality that can claim a universal agreement. But this one has
received the same formulation in almost all traditions, namely,
that it is only in accepting silence that people can come to know
their own spirit, and only in abandonment to an infinite depth
of silence that they can be revealed to the source of their spirit
in which multiplicity and division disappear. Modern people are
often threatened by silence, what T. S. Eliot called "the growing
terror of nothing to think about," and everyone has to face this
fear when they begin to meditate.

First, we must confront with some shame the chaotic din of

a mind ravaged by so much exposure to trivia and distraction. Persevering through this in fidelity to the mantra, we then encounter a darker level of consciousness, of repressed fears and anxieties. The radical simplicity of the mantra clears this too. But our first inclination is always to retreat from the dawn of self-knowledge and, as Walter Hilton very graphically expressed it, "This is not surprising for if a man came home to his house and found nothing but a smoking fire and a nagging wife, he would quickly run out again."

In entering upon these first two levels, of surface distractions and subconscious anxiety, we risk being bruised. But in entering into the next, into our own silence, we risk everything, for we risk our very being: "So I said to my soul, 'Be still.'" The stillness of mind and body to which the mantra guides us is a preparation for entering this silence, and for our progression through the spheres of silence to see with wonder the light of our own spirit, and to know that light as something beyond our spirit and yet the source of it. This is a pilgrimage through our spheres of silence that we undertake in faith, putting our entire trust in what is only a dim apprehension of the authentic, the real, yet confident in doing so because it is authentic.

In saying the mantra, we lay down our life for the sake of him we have not yet seen. Blessed are they who believe and act on their belief though they have not yet seen. In saying the mantra we are plunged into a silence that explores our infinite poverty of mind and spirit, revealing our absolute dependence on another. We are led from depth to depth of purifying simplification until, having contacted the very ground of our being, we find the life we laid down and the self we surrendered in the Other.

St. Paul claimed to carry the dying of Christ within himself, and it was because of the authenticity of that perception that his witness to Christ was radiant with risen life. It is precisely in this dying of Jesus that we all participate. St. Luke's Gospel emphasizes that Jesus called upon all to renounce self and to take up their cross daily. To that call we respond when we meditate every day. We mislead ourselves and others if we try to play down the extremity of the Christian vocation and the total demand it makes. If we have been directed by the Spirit to undertake this pilgrimage, and every Christian is chosen to do so, then it must be with the mature understanding of what is at stake. As we enter the silence within us, having allowed ourselves to become aware of its presence in the first place, we are entering a void in which we are unmade. We cannot remain the person we were or thought we were. But we are, in fact, not being destroyed but awakened to the eternally fresh source of our being. We become aware that we are being created, that we are springing from the Creator's hand and returning to him in love.

In the silence, we are being prepared for this awakening which is an encounter with the fullness and the splendor of Jesus in that fully awakened state to which the resurrection led him, because no one comes to the Father except through the Son in whom all creation comes into being. But even if we know intellectually that this is the purpose of the silence, at the time our actual experience is of the void. In the beginning, we know reduction, not expansion, a shedding of qualities and a contraction to the point of pure being in pure poverty of spirit, a cataclysmic simplicity.

The Christian carries this dying within him as he goes about his daily routine, not in a self-dramatizing or self-obsessed way, but with a joyful awareness that more and more deeply suffuses his whole being, that the degree to which he dies to himself in this void is the degree to which he is revivified in the transcendent life of the completely free man, Jesus. "Though our outward humanity is in decay, yet day by day we are inwardly renewed." Within the structure of our daily life, this inward renewal of which St. Paul speaks is the purpose and fruit of our twice-daily meditation. We are literally made new in the fact of entering into the ever deeper centers of being, and of knowing ever more fully the harmony of all our qualities and energies in that ultimate center of our being which is the center and source of all being, the center of the Trinitarian love. "When anyone is united to Christ," Paul wrote to the Corinthians, "there is a new world."

As the Christian enters into the cycle of death and resurrection more thoroughly, he becomes more aware of its universal truth, that it is the model of all being. He begins to appreciate what mystery is. In order to become fully opened to the force of this universal cycle, we need to understand that it is completed at every level of every life, and in all of the countless ways in which we can examine or apprehend the meaning of our own life. It is, for example, the cycle upon which each half-hour of meditation is based, a death to the possessiveness and triviality occupying our ego and a rising to the liberty and significance that dawn when we find ourselves by looking fully at the Other. It is, too, the cycle upon which a whole lifetime of prayer can be seen on a larger scale. We are dying and rising to new life every day as we participate in the evolution of God's plan for each of his creatures.

Yet it is also true that there is only one death and one rising, that which Jesus underwent for all creation. The Word proceeds from silence and it returns to the unfathomable silence and limitless love of the Father, the cycle of issuing and return upon which every life cycle in creation is based, the cycle in which creation exists at every moment, could it but see this with a pure heart. But the Word does not return under the same conditions. In revealing himself to humanity in the depths of a person's own being, which are the depths of God, the Word fulfills the purpose of the Father from whose silence he and, in him, creation proceed. This is the purpose of our being of which we read a thousand times in Paul's words to the Ephesians and yet can never fully fathom:

In Christ he chose us before the world was founded, to be dedicated, to be without blemish in his sight, to be full of love; and he destined us, such as was his will and pleasure, to be accepted as his children through Jesus Christ, in order that the glory of his gracious gift, so graciously bestowed upon us in his Beloved, might redound to his praise.

It is a stupefying claim that our meaning is somehow involved in the meaning of God himself, and we need to have the courage that only utter simplicity affords in order to accept it. No egoism or complexity can awaken to this revelation: "Unless you become like little children, you cannot enter the kingdom of heaven." We know that this claim is authentic because of our communion with the Word, the Son. All things and all people return to the Father through the Son and of the Son. St. John tells us that: "Through him all things came to be; no single thing was created without him." So just as he is the prime and ultimate expression of the Father, Jesus is also the hinge upon which the universe and all being swings back to the Father, its source. It is through our incorporation in the body of Christ in this swing-back to the Father that we are destined to be accepted as children of God.

In its essential significance, the aim of meditation is just this: the realization of our total incorporation in Jesus Christ, in the cycle of his utterance by, and return to, the Father. The qualities we need in this fundamental encounter between ourselves and the ground of our being are attentiveness and receptivity. In order to realize our complete incorporation with the Word, we have not only to listen to its silence, the silence within us, but also to allow the cycle of its life to be completed in us and to lead us into the depth of its silence. There in the silence of the Word we share his experience of hearing himself eternally spoken by the Father.

This is why the life of Jesus is of such meaning and why Scripture's record of his life is of such value. The experience of Jesus of Nazareth in awakening to himself, entering the spheres of silence within himself, finding his own Spirit and the source of his spirit, this experience is the experience of every person reborn in spirit. And it is, within the unimaginable design of the Father, the self-same experience. The wonder of creation is found, not in a succession of awakenings, but in the single all-inclusive awakening of Jesus, the Son, to the Father.

Our language is wholly inadequate and our thought too self-conscious to reflect the simplicity and actuality of this cycle of dying and rising. But it is not language for thought we need. We need only to become aware of the mystery within us, the silence in which we see our own spirit. Our path into this silence is the one little word of the mantra. —WS 30–35

Life and Resurrection

Any of us can wander off on diversions, into distractions, triviality, and self-importance. The great power of liberty and confidence that permeates our life, however, is that we do have a way back to the straight way, to simplicity and other-centerlines. Our way back is simply the love of Jesus that is always present to us, in our own heart, not as something we have either to earn or conjure up — but as something that simply is and is so simply that it underpins and surrounds us in the root of our being. It lives us into being and cannot leave us until we have freely accepted the gift of being it bestows.
—LH 129–30

It is only too easy to anesthetize ourselves, to be so soaked in our own images or self-reflection that we just drift along, hovering or floating in a realm of self-conscious piety. But it is also possible to take the journey to reality, to be led by Christ the enlightened one into the great awakening to his Father and to realize our vocation to sanctity. By ourselves we could not make the journey. But we are not by ourselves because we are "in the Spirit." Nor can this experience even be understood just as our own experience. Our vision is the vision of Jesus, and our knowledge of God is a oneness with his knowledge.

—LH 130

Meditation is focused right in the heart, right in the center of the Christian mystery. And the Christian mystery can be penetrated only if we enter into the mystery of death and resurrection. That is the essential message of Jesus. No one can be a follower of Jesus unless he leaves self behind. The person who would find his life must be ready to lose it. And in all the parables drawn from nature Jesus gives, the seed must fall into the ground and die, or it remains alone.

What we do in meditation and in the lifelong process of meditation is to refine our perception down to the single focal point, which is Christ. Christ is our way, our goal, and our guide. But he is our goal only in the sense that once we are wholly with him, wholly at one with him, we pass with him to the Father. In meditation we come to that necessary single-pointedness and find it is Christ.   —MC 13

We celebrate Easter liturgically over a few days, but we discover its meaning only in a lifetime. Each year I hear these words of St. Paul read out during the ceremonies and their significance seems to become both sharper and more real, urgent and yet more mysterious, each year. By baptism we were buried with him, and lay dead, in order that, as Christ was raised from the dead in the splendor of the Father, so also we might set our feet upon the new path of life.

To know this is to be a Christian, not just a member of a church or sect but a joyful personal disciple. It is to know that this new path of life is already opened up for us because of the energies set free among all humanity by the resurrection. From our point of view we may see only the same tired, worn, old paths, but if this resurrection energy has touched us, if we have touched it in our hearts, the new path of life stands out brilliant and dominant, transcending all the old ways. As the snows of winter melted in our garden here a carpet of brown and withered leaves from last fall was exposed. As we started to rake them away we found that the earth was covered with young green shoots pushing up from the earth with an irrepressible energy — the energy of life. We have to penetrate beyond the surface to make contact with the new life of the resurrection.

The resurrection is the eternal sign of our invitation to share in the glory, the complete realization of Christ. Just what does this new resurrection-life mean? Does it have personal meaning for each one of us, or is it like a news item that everyone talks about and no one feels involved in? We find the answer, I think, in the New Testament accounts of the resurrection. They all make it transparently clear that the risen Jesus could be seen and recognized only with the eyes of faith. "She turned around and saw Jesus standing there, but did not recognize him. . . . Jesus said, 'Mary.' She turned to him and said 'Rabbuni!' (which is Hebrew for 'My Master')."

In the profoundly real and symbolic atmosphere of this encounter there is a marvelously condensed account of the human response to the resurrection. We hear and see the good news, but until the moment that it engages our absolute attention, by name, we fail to recognize it. When we do, all thought of self evaporates in the overwhelming joy of the reality, so much greater than us, that can call us into itself. Mary is described as "turning" twice, in this brief episode. For all of us there is this twofold conversion that unfolds throughout a lifetime, the total conversion that demands absolute harmony of mind and heart.

Each of us needs this clarified vision that enables us to recognize what we see. Without this new dimension of faith we can only fail to see and to recognize the risen Christ within the creation he now pervades. Finding the power of vision which lets us see what is there, lets us see what is, requires of us the wisdom to penetrate the shell of reality, to go beyond appearances. This does not mean rejecting the ordinary or cultivating an esoteric essential spirituality. Far from it. To go that route would be to remain locked at the most superficial of all levels of reality: the vanity of the self-centered consciousness, the egoism of the alienated "me." Penetrating the appearance of things means rediscovering in childlike wonder the divine and mysterious correspondence between appearance and meaning between the mortal and the immortal. In the Christian vision of eternal life — which means full realization of all potentiality — nothing is rejected or wasted. Even our most fragile and ephemeral dimension, our body, is to be "saved" from the entropic processes that so frighten us: so that as St. Paul said, "Our mortal part may be absorbed into life immortal."

We need the wisdom to search into the depths of things. We also need a deepening sensitivity to a dimension of reality which can be revealed only to those who want to see, who are humble enough to cry out with the blind beggar of the gospel, "Lord, that I may see." It is only the blindly arrogant who claim to see enough. Those who are beginning to see are aware of how much more their vision of faith needs to be purified. They know that no one can see God and live. The more we see God the further our self-consciousness contracts and our ego evaporates. To see God is to be absorbed into God. To have the eye of our heart opened by the process of his love is to lose our very sense of the "I" who sees. This is the sensitivity, the delicacy of spiritual refinement we need in order to see the risen Christ. It is the gentle delicacy that follows the cataclysm of death. It is the spirit of fully selfless love that does not flinch from being transformed into the beloved. What we shall be has not yet been disclosed, but we know that when it is disclosed we shall be like him, because we shall see him as he is. There is an immortal power, the "strength" of God, in this sensitivity. And that is why we cannot enter the new vision without finding a harmony with the basic structure of reality, without being sensitive to the truth that the underpinning reality of everything we see is God. It is in this sense that meditation is rightly called a way of wisdom, a way of vision.

Wisdom is more than the knowledge derived from accumulated experience. Vision is more than the power to visualize. To be wise we must learn to know with the heart. To see we must learn to see with the eyes of the heart — with love.

—PC 89–92

Our Guide

In the Christian vision we are led to this source of our being by a guide, and our guide is Jesus, the fully realized man, the man wholly open to God. As we meditate each day we may not recognize our guide. That is why the Christian journey is always a journey of faith. But as we approach the center of our being, as we enter our heart, we find that we are greeted by our guide, greeted by the one who has led us. We are welcomed by the person who calls each one of us into personal fullness of being.

The consequences or results of meditation are just this fullness of life — harmony, oneness, and energy, a divine energy that we find in our own heart, in our own spirit. That is the energy that is love.

—MC 11

The real meaning of faith is: openness, perseverance in wakefulness, commitment to the pilgrimage. The word for faith (*pistis*), so common in the gospel sayings of Jesus, nowhere in his teaching meant "belief" or "conviction." It carries instead the sense

of "trust," "faithfulness," and personal loyalty. To follow Jesus
was not merely to have an intellectual understanding about him
but to experience his personal revelation and the dimension of
spirit his person opened up for us — to experience this at the
center of our lives to the point of union with him and so ultimately with the Father. "He who believes [has *pistis*] in me,
believes not in me, but in the one who sent me." The openness
and steadiness of this faith in Jesus leads us to the transcendence of every human limitation separating us from the Father's
love, the source and goal of our being. He is the Way. But we
do not enter on to the way except through faith. Once we have
entered upon it, it will progressively draw more and more of
our being into itself. It will seem as if it is integrating and unifying us simply in order to possess us and fill us more perfectly.
Out of this central Christian experience flows the abundance of
joy and hope proclaimed by the gospel and a rootedness in ourselves and the reality of the redemptive power of love in human
life. It does not demand merely our emotional or our intellectual faculties but the whole person offered as a living sacrifice
in the praise of heart and mind. Through the wonder of this
wholeness a complete revolution is effected in us: "When anyone is united to Christ there is a New World; the old order has
gone and a new order has already begun."

As the new world reveals itself more and more fully, we begin
to see the mystery as truly a personal one. Once a Christian has
entered upon this pilgrimage he or she becomes a vital force
through which the personal communication of Jesus is made.
Each one of us is summoned to participate in this work of
union. If we say, "This is too much for me" or "I don't know
what to do," we are evading the call. All we have to do is to
accept the gift we have been given: the gift of the life of the
risen Lord, which can transform us and renew us in our turning toward him with our whole consciousness fully awake to its
power. The courage we need for this is the courage to become

truly silent, deeply unified. It is our mantra taking us beyond the constrictions of language and imagination that leads us into the unbounded reality of the Lord Jesus. Our twice-daily meditations and during these times our absolute fidelity to the mantra as the one occupation of our mind and heart — this is our lifeline with the center to which we are traveling and out of which flows the abundant power of love to remain steady on the way of centrality. And the center where all lines converge is Jesus.

— LH 57–58

When we are preparing for Christmas, we should try to reflect in the light of meditation about the essential, the spiritual significance of the Incarnation. God became man so that man might become God. This theme is the constant conviction of the Eastern churches and the teaching of the Greek Fathers.

By the Incarnation God has touched our lives in Jesus, and the great importance of the feast of Christmas is that it is the celebration of our humanity, redeemed by being touched by God. God assumes the mortality of the human condition in Jesus so that we can burst through the bonds of death in him. Indeed, he bursts through all the chains that keep us bound by the earth. What we learn from his life is that the destiny of each one of us is to begin to live our lives fully now, in our present earthly, mortal condition. To live our lives now, as free men and women, not bound by fear or enchained by desire, but utterly in harmony with the liberating power of God's own energy. This energy of God cannot be bounded by any human limitation. It is the eternal life source, not just constantly renewed in each one of us but always expanding in each one of us. And our invitation, our destiny, is to place our lives in complete harmony with this divine energy. And so the Christian experience cannot be contained by any set of propositions, by any library of books, by any formulas or creeds. It can be adequately expressed only in the human experience of Jesus himself. He alone, of all human beings, was able to say to God, "Abba Father."

The mystery of the Incarnation and the sheer wonder of the Christian proclamation of truth is that Christ shares his experience with each one of us. And he actively invites each one of us to enter into his own experience of the Father. He invites us not just to make some sort of intellectual assent or volitional intention. He invites us *to share,* to share with his experience in all its fullness, to be carried away by the infinite thrust of his energy as he knows the Father and loves the Father, and as he in his turn is known and loved infinitely. And this is what we are called to; every one of us.

In meditation we develop full attention, full commitment because what we set out for is to enter the eternal moment of God's self-communication in Jesus. We are called not just to consider this but to share it, to enter into it at the very depth of our being. And the result for us is deep, supreme, unshakeable joy. Our minds and hearts are expanded beyond all isolation into oneness, into union. The way is the way of daily fidelity.

Wherever we are on the path — whether we are just beginning and meditating twice every day for twenty minutes, or whether we have been on the path for some time and we meditate for thirty minutes or meditate three times a day — wherever we are, all that is required is that we give ourselves totally now to our commitment. It seems, when we begin, that this is asking a lot, but the feast of Christmas reminds us that God in his gift to us did not just give us a lot, he gives us everything of himself in Jesus. Somehow we must understand that, and we must understand it in the silence of our own heart. We must understand it in the eternal silence of God.

And so when we meditate each morning and evening, we each of us receive, as fully as we are now able to, the gift of God in Jesus. To receive it requires a generosity on our part that is not less than the generosity of God. That is why we must say our mantra with the greatest attention we can, with the greatest love we can. The words of Jesus constantly inspire us to deepen our generosity:

"Father, I desire that these who are thy gift to me may be with me where I am, so that they may look upon my glory, which thou hast given me because thou didst love me before the world began. O righteous Father, although the world does not know thee, I know thee and these know that thou didst send me. I made thy name known to them and will make it known so that the love thou hadst for me may be in them, and I may be in them."   —WU 100–102

SPIRIT

It is our conviction that the central message of the New Testament is that there is really only one prayer, and that this prayer is the prayer of Christ. It is a prayer that continues in our hearts day and night. I can describe it only as the stream of love that flows constantly between Jesus and his Father. This stream of love is the Holy Spirit.

Again it is our conviction that it is the most important task for any fully human life that we should become as open as possible to this stream of love. We have to allow this prayer to become our prayer; we have to enter into the experience of being swept out of ourselves, beyond ourselves into this wonderful prayer of Jesus — this great cosmic river of love.

In order for us to do this we learn a way that is a way of silence, of stillness, and this by a discipline that is most demanding. It is as though we have to create a space within ourselves that will allow this higher consciousness — the consciousness of the prayer of Jesus — to envelop us in this powerful mystery. We have got used to thinking of prayer in terms of "my prayer" or "my praise" of God, and it requires a complete rethinking of

our attitude to prayer if we are going to come to see it as a way
through Jesus, with Jesus, and in Jesus.   — MC x–xi

The first step in personhood then is to allow ourselves to be
loved. It was to facilitate this that the Holy Spirit was sent into
the human heart, to touch it, to awaken it, to draw our minds
into its redemptive light. The sending of the Spirit was a resurrection event. It continues as freshly today as it did "late that
Sunday evening" [as St. John tells us], when the disciples were
together behind locked doors and Jesus came and breathed on
them saying: "Receive the Holy Spirit."   — WS 37

We begin with a dim awareness of the stirring of the Spirit in
our heart, the presence of Another by which we know ourselves.
In awakening to its full reality, in listening to our heart, we
awaken to the living proof of our faith justifying that first dim
awareness, that first hope. And, as St. Paul told the Romans:
"This proof is the ground of hope. Such a hope is no mockery
because God's love has flooded our inmost heart through the
Holy Spirit he has given us."   — WS 38

3

Being with God

In John Main's theology and view of human nature prayer has the highest value. Quality of life and personal integrity depend on it, as does our salvation. Of the many types of prayer that have been classified as Christian, his principal concern was the "pure prayer" of the monastic tradition that became identified with "contemplation" and that John Main usually called "meditation." Yet for John Main prayer in the fullest Christian understanding could never be reduced to types, forms, methods, or techniques.

When he began to teach meditation John Main found both a hunger and receptiveness, usually from lay people, and often an angry resistance, usually from clergy, who, he said, were the most difficult audiences he had to address. This changed over time as they came to a better understanding of his teaching and saw its fruits in the lives of people who followed it. But at first he ran headlong into the assumption, unconsciously reinforced in seminaries and parishes, that prayer is primarily a communion with God. Teaching from the mystical tradition John Main asserts the conviction that prayer is not essentially about talking to God or thinking about God but being with God. Christian faith, he believes, makes this explicit because the human con-

sciousness of Jesus has ushered in a "new age of Presence" that gives us a capacity for communion hitherto unrealized.

Because we no longer think about ourselves, the prayer of silence creates the inner space that allows the "prayer of Jesus" to envelop us. Whisked beyond self-consciousness in the mind of Christ that is turned wholly to the Father, the ground of being and source of creation, we too become open to that transcendent mystery of God. Prayer in this sense is also an openness of heart, which means that at the deep center of our own being we experience the life of Jesus at its most personal intensity. Prayer is an awakening to his presence within us, to his awakening to the Father.

Although all this might sound abstract, meditation shows it to be of the highest and most immediate order of reality. Prayer for John Main is not speculation about God or fantasy relationships with God. It is about the transforming experience of reciprocal presence. Prayer changes the world because it first changes us. If we try to use prayer to change the world to our own specifications without being prepared to be changed ourselves, we are living in the realm of superstition, in retreat from our own fears and anxieties. He believed passionately that the Christian understanding of prayer today must mature if Christianity is to evolve and play its destined role as a spiritual authority in the world.

PRAYER

Presence

The reality Jesus has uncovered for us is the new age of Presence. It demands a correspondingly new understanding of how we share in the Trinitarian mystery. Because of the new Christic consciousness we can understand in a way that is disturbingly personal and universal that we do not so much exist in relation to God as subsist in God — he is the ground of our being. We are called to know and to know fully, not just notionally, that nothing can be outside the ground of all being that God is. And so, in the light of Christ, prayer is not talking-to, but being-with. —PC 55–56

The essence of Christian prayer is not dialogue but union, oneness. I think most of us know this in our heart of hearts. We know from our own experience that if we see prayer as dialogue, "dialoguing with God," it frequently ends up as monologue.

The tradition that we follow as Benedictine monks calls us both to understand and to experience our prayer as silent communion within our own heart. Union brings us to communion, that is, to a oneness discovered within ourselves but which leads us to oneness with God and to openness with all. It is a communion that is indescribably enriching, because it takes us right out of ourselves, beyond ourselves into union with all, with the All, with God. Unity, union, communion is the threefold growth of a Christian.

The experience of prayer is the experience of coming into full union with the energy that created the universe. What Christianity has to proclaim to the world is that that energy is love and it is the wellspring that gives each one of us the creative power to be the person we are called to be — a person rooted and founded in love. —MC 20

We have come to think of prayer largely as our movement to God, as an activity that we are responsible for, a duty we perform to please God or to appease him. There can be an element of charm, of childish sincerity in this, but true prayer eschews the sentimental. We have been summoned to a spiritual maturity in which, as St. Peter tells us, "we are alive with the life of

God." Now if he, St. Paul, and the New Testament as a whole deserve to be taken seriously, we are led to say that prayer is something greater than our talking to God, or imagining God, or imagining holy thoughts. Indeed as St. Paul said, this cannot be a real explanation of prayer if it is true that we do not even know how to pray. But as he goes on to say, "the Spirit is pleading for us in our inmost being beyond words, beyond thoughts, beyond images, with sighs too deep for words."

Prayer then, is the life of the Spirit of Jesus within our human heart: the Spirit through whose anointing we are incorporated in the Body of Christ and by which, in turn, we are returning fully awake to the Father. We are praying when we are awakening to the presence of the Spirit in our heart. If this is so, there can be no forms or methods of prayer. There is one prayer, the stream of love between the Spirit of the risen Christ and his Father, in which we are incorporated. If this is so, there is no part-time or partial prayer as if the Spirit were not always alive in our hearts. But there are times, our twice-daily meditation, when we make a complete turn of consciousness toward this ever present reality. There comes a level of awakening — to which St. Paul was clearly directing the Thessalonians when he told them "to pray without ceasing" — when our awareness of this reality is constant throughout the most diverse activities or concerns.   — WS 38–39

We can be so used to being compulsively busy in our prayers, and multiplying our prayers, that just becoming silent is quite a problem for us. And so we have always got to be aware so that we do not just float off into that "holy-dozy" sort of state of pious dozing, which John Cassian calls the "pernicious peace" or the "lethal sleep."

I want to elaborate a bit on this because I want you to have a clear understanding of it when it happens. There is a real danger here because the religious person likes this pious religiosity, a feeling of being, as I say, slightly stoned in a religious way; but this can become a half-living limbo state. Do not underestimate the danger: in my experience, certainly among the religious I have met over the years, people can get stranded in this limbo where they just float and do not make any further progress at all in prayer. They never become fully alive. They do not become fully awake to the presence within, which is a waking experience of the living God.

At the root of the unreality is what one could call "unspiritual religiosity." It boils down to an evasion of our responsibility to enter fully into the present moment. I am sure you know the great phrase of St. Irenaeus that the "glory of God is man fully alive." To be fully alive means we have to respond totally to the reality of the here and now. This is a bigger problem than you might imagine because it is apparently so much easier for Christians to opt for the past. So many Christians seem to prefer a backward projection into the historical life of Christ and to be constantly locked in it. They lose contact with the living Christ, the risen Christ, who lives now in our hearts. That seems to me to be one of the great Christian dangers: reducing your prayer to thinking about the historical life of Jesus. What we must do instead is to encounter the living Lord in our own hearts and then find him elsewhere: in our lives and relationships in the living word of Scripture. There is a serious danger to face here just as it can be one of the dangers, for example, about the Stations of the Cross. It is one of the dangers of the sort of piety that gets locked into "meditation" upon the historical events of the life of Jesus. That Jesus lived historically is, of course, of supreme importance. I do not deny that for a moment! But the essence of the New Testament is that the Lord Jesus lives. The Risen Christ lives in my heart and in your heart. It is with this dimension of his vital and vitalizing presence within me and within you that we must come to read the account of his historical life. —AW 48–49

In our prayer then, we let God be; we rejoice in his being as he is; we do not try to manipulate him, to harangue him, or to flatter him. We do not dispel him with our clever words and formulae but we worship him, that is, we acknowledge his value and worth and in doing this we discover that we, created in his image, share in his value and worth as children of God.

—WS 76

The immediacy, the urgency of the Christian revelation is that all this is a present reality, established in the center of the human condition, demanding only that we realize it. This is why meditation is neither a backward glance nor a timorous projection forward but rather combines the old and the new in the glory of the eternal present — the "perpetual now." And it is this element in meditation that makes the meditator a truly contemporary person, fully open and alive to the ever present creative power of God sustaining the universe in being from moment to moment. The liberty to "move with the times," to recognize the changing needs and circumstances of the community or society around us, is the fruit of stability at the center of our being.

It often seems to many people that prayer is an introspective state and that the meditator is someone going into himself to the exclusion of the people and creation around him, that he is socially irrelevant. Nothing could be further from the truth. Not only is the timeless contemplative vision the necessary basis for contemporary action but it is the essential condition for a fully human response to life — to the richness, the unpredictability, the sheer given quality of life. The persistent temptation to which we have to be constantly alert is that we opt for the half-life that denies the present reality of the incarnation: either seeking all value in the world or all in spirit. Because of Christ alive and active in the human heart and people's social relationships, the two are gloriously interfused.   —LH 65

Forms of Prayer

Walter Hilton is a very good witness to the truth that there is no antipathy as it were between contemplative prayer, vocal prayer, liturgical prayer. He does trace a kind of progressive development through these forms but not in the sense that we ever get to a stage in our life when we have gone beyond liturgical prayer or vocal prayer. The development he really sees is a growth in the delight with which one enters into whatever form is appropriate at any time. And all these forms of prayer are, of course, complementary, provided that we know them as they really are: as entrances into the eternal prayer of Jesus which is his loving return to the Father. At all times in our lives all the various streams of prayer are coming together and binding us ever more closely to the Lord Jesus in the universal ocean of his prayer.   —CM 38

Our call is to commit ourselves to the absolute God, to the one who is. There is no ultimate evasion of the truth that we can only commit ourselves absolutely. How do we learn commitment? What does Jesus tell us? He tells us to worship. The Hebrew word for worship derives from the root word "to serve." Jesus teaches us that "the worshipers whom the Father wants must worship in spirit and truth." The worshiper is one who serves, that is, one who is absolutely at the disposition of his Lord. Absolutely. We must serve in spirit, that is, from the depth of our being, not at the surface, not using other people's insights, but worshiping from the ground of our own experience, our own unique being. We must serve in truth, beyond all illusion, while accepting the reality of God and the reality of ourselves as we are. The theological basis of Christian meditation is that the essential reality of prayer is the prayer of Jesus. In the same way that there is only one essential Christian prayer, the prayer of Christ himself, so there is only one

Christian worship, the communion we have through Christ in
the Trinitarian love. Each member of the Trinity wholly *at the
service* of the other. Entry into this worship can be found only
at the heart of creation, that is, through the human worship of
Christ, wholly at the disposition of the Father and receiving the
Father's love, absolutely.

If we are to realize the full potential of the gift of life we
need to see that our destiny is the same as Christ's. Our destiny is to be wholly at the service of God, to worship him in
the depth of our being, to worship him in spirit and truth.
Through such worship it is also our destiny to receive his love
fully. The humble ordinary task of saying the mantra, and saying it faithfully, is simply our way of entering this worship, of
putting ourselves wholly at the disposition of God. Scripture returns again and again to the simplicity and clarity of the state of
commitment, and how far removed this state is from the mind-
made substitute of thought and language. It is when we learn
to be simple that we enter into the absolute love of God. To be
simple is to be like Christ, an unambiguous yes to God.

—WU 95–96

The profound Christian reality is that the "Way" is not merely
a historical tradition but is something much greater: our own
lived experience of the present reality of the risen Lord Jesus,
the Christ.

The wonder is that this is our Way. In Luke's narratives
there is the motif of Christ's journey to Jerusalem. Indeed, the
whole of his account of Jesus' ministry is framed as his progress
toward the holy city, his being en route to his great priestly destiny, which was that moment in his life when he was to burst
the bonds of every limitation implicit in his incarnation — to
become, as St. Paul tells us, "life-giving spirit." In Luke's account, the sign of a person's response to Jesus as he journeyed

to Jerusalem was whether or not that person turned around, changed direction, and followed him.

During his ministry, the "Way" was the journey Jesus followed as his pilgrimage through love and suffering to his Father. But after the perfection of his love in the suffering of the cross, he reached the goal of his pilgrimage and was glorified in his return to the Father's right hand. And so it is that in chapter 14 of his Gospel St. John tells us that the Way now is the person of Jesus himself.

Christian prayer, then, has the essentially dynamic quality of the mystery of Jesus himself because it is an encounter and entry into the person of Jesus, who is the way to the Father. The Christian pilgrimage is a turning, a conversion, a following of Christ and a journey with Christ. It is never complacent or self-satisfied. And its essential insight is that our full meaning lies beyond ourselves. Salvation, within this terminology, is being on the way, being turned toward the dynamic power of Jesus and being taken up in him to the Father. Salvation is entering the kingdom of heaven that is within us.

One of the great perils of the pilgrimage is that we talk so much about it and so cleverly imagine ourselves in it that we actually fail to tread it, to put one foot in front of the other. I have spoken to you of this danger often enough. It is the *pax perniciosa* (false peace), mere religiosity or "holy floating." We are all in continuous need of that quality that St. Paul speaks of in chapter one of 1 Thessalonians — the quality *of hupomone,* sometimes translated as patience, sometimes as endurance, but best of all, it seems to me, as fortitude. This is the courage to keep on the Way with growing fidelity to our twice-daily meditation — times in the day when we quite explicitly put everything aside so that we may enter the journey of the Lord with our full attention. Let no one deceive you into thinking that this explicit "work" is not necessary. Of course, we are always on the Way, always journeying with him. It is the condition of all creatures and all creation. But we are called to a full, mature, and personal awareness of it. And just as he stood aside from his ministry of healing, teaching, and preaching to be alone with his Father, wholly turned toward his presence at the center of his being, so too must we follow in this Way. The gospels clearly testify to his practice of withdrawing from his active ministry and the crowds that followed him to pray in silence and solitude. But this was in addition to the normal religious practice of his day he would have followed, of the three regular periods of prayer during the day. The practical, daily structure of his life was, then, provided by his faithful commitment to prayer.

So, too, our life. The structure of our life must be based on our regular, silent attentiveness to the source of our life — if we are to accept that "fullness of life" Jesus offers. After all that one can say about prayer and however wonderful the mystery seems to our mind, it comes down to this: fidelity to our twice daily meditation and, within the time of meditation, complete fidelity to the word — the mantra that leads us on the Way. The beauty of the gospels, the delight of creation, the concerns of our life — everything must be placed on the altar of the living sacrifice of praise we offer by saying our mantra. By saying it to the exclusion of all thought and imagination we will be led into a depth of silence on the other side of all distraction. In this silence, Jesus, the Word, is rooted in our hearts; we are made one with him; we journey with him to the Father.   — LH 46–48

MEDITATION

If philosophy, as Plato said, begins in wonder, meditation, for John Main, begins with an overwhelming sense of reverence. This remains the best preparation for meditation. The loss of a sense of the sacred, including the sacredness of our own hu-

manity, poses a great danger to the world. And therefore growth in spiritual awareness is today's highest priority. For this to be accomplished, we must recover the experience and meaning of silence.

Silence has psychological aspects, of course, but John Main is interested in the spiritual discovery awaiting us if we enter the silence that is within us. What we experience in that eternal silence is the love of God. And once experienced we know that love is the "supreme reality."

Simplicity is another great challenge because of the inveterate temptation to complicate things. The mantra itself meets and resolves these challenges, but the mantra is a great challenge too. That is why it is important to understand from the beginning that the process of growth that the mantra launches is organic, not mechanical. John Main showed how this process of growth allows time for the mantra to become rooted before the prayer of Jesus flourishes and flowers. The challenge of faith is to repeat lovingly, not mechanically. We must learn to see the times of meditation not as our own times of prayer but as time for the prayer of Jesus to expand in and through us.

John Main's essential concern is to help people get started. He is therefore reluctant to describe in detail more "advanced" stages of the practice of meditation as this could easily pander to mere curiosity, while what people need is to jump in and to learn from their own experience. His teaching dispels the misconceptions or fears that prevent people from doing that — the idea, for example, that meditation is foreign, esoteric, or a dangerous technique.

Silence

The mystery of our relationship with God is one that embraces such a vast canvas that only by developing our capacity for awe-filled and reverential silence will we ever be able to appreciate even a fraction of its wonder. We know that God is intimately with us, and we know also that he is infinitely beyond us. It is only through deep and liberating silence that we can reconcile the polarities of this mysterious paradox. And the liberation that we experience in silent prayer is precisely liberation from the inevitably distorting effects of language when we begin to experience God's intimate and transcendent dominion within us.   —WS 7

There is also the extraordinary knowledge that it is our destiny, the destiny of each one of us, to enter into God's dynamism of oneness in complete peace and total silence, and in that peace and silence to know ourselves loved. After this we know forever that love is the supreme reality. The peace of this entry into God we can accept easily enough. But it is the silence we all find so much more difficult. As we enter ever deeper into the depths of silence, we are tempted to return to the shallows, to postpone the ultimate leap, the total act of faith. And perhaps we are right to be hesitant, because once made that leap is made forever. There is no turning back from the leap of "all or nothing."   —HC 73

The all-important aim in Christian meditation is to allow God's mysterious and silent presence within us to become more and more not only a reality, but *the* reality in our lives; to let it become that reality which gives meaning to everything we do, everything we are.   —WS 3

First we must understand the Christian context of meditation. I am using the term "meditation" in this instance synonymously with such terms as "contemplation," "contemplative prayer," "meditative prayer," and so on. The essential context of meditation is to be found in the fundamental relationship of our lives, the relationship that we have as creatures with God, our Cre-

ator. But most of us have to take a preliminary step before we
can begin to appreciate the full wonder and glorious mystery of
this fundamental relationship. Most of us have to get into touch
with ourselves first, to get into a full relationship with ourselves
before we can turn openly to our relationship with God. Putting
this another way, we can say that we have first to find, expand,
and experience our own capacity for peace, for serenity, and for
harmony before we can begin to appreciate our God and Father,
who is the author of all harmony and serenity.

Meditation is the very simple process by which we prepare
ourselves in the first instance, to be at peace with ourselves so
that we are capable of appreciating the peace of the Godhead
within us. The view of meditation that many people are encouraged to take as a means of relaxation, of retaining inner
peacefulness throughout the pressures of modern urban life, is
not essentially wrong in itself. But if this is all it is seen as being, the view is very limited because, as we become more and
more relaxed in ourselves, and the longer we meditate, the more
we become aware that the source of our newfound calm in our
daily lives is precisely the life of God within us. The degree of
peace we possess is directly proportional to our awareness of
this fact of life, a fact of human consciousness common to every
man and every woman in the world. But to realize this fact as
a present reality in our lives, we have to decide that we want to
be at peace. This is the reason for the psalmist's saying: "Be still
and know that I am God."   — WS 1–2

The most important thing to know about meditation is how
to meditate. It is also important I suppose to know why you
should meditate, but in the first place you must know what to
do. Let me remind you of this again so that you are as clear as
possible in your minds about it. Choose a place that is as quiet
as you can find. As far as posture is concerned, the basic rule
is to sit with your spine upright. Sit down, either on the floor

or in an upright chair, and keep your spine as erect as possible. Close your eyes gently.

To meditate you need to take a word, and the word I suggest to you is *Maranatha*. Simply, gently repeat that word in silence in your heart, in the depths of your being, and continue repeating it. Listen to it as a sound. Say it; articulate it in silence, clearly, but listen to it as a sound. If you can, you must meditate every morning and every evening. I think it is true to say that you will never learn to meditate unless you do meditate every day. You need simply to put that time slot aside.   —WU 1

Seeing how prayer of petition and prayer of intercession fit in with this type of prayer is a very topical question. I think that a lot of people see meditation as a kind of stoic exercise in which you are concerned with your own growth in holiness or in wisdom to the exclusion of all other relationships and concerns. It is necessary to understand clearly that meditative prayer is not the only form of prayer there is. As I have said, vocal and liturgical prayer forms both have their proper place.

But when we come to meditate we open ourselves fully to God's abiding presence within us, in the simple faith that that presence is the All-in-all. Our hearts are fully open to this love. And our hearts are, of course, fully open to his scrutiny. He knows exactly all our concerns, all our loves, all our fears before we articulate them. And in this well called "prayer of faith" we do not articulate them but offer them to him in faithful silence. A person who meditates, then, is not some heartless pursuer of wisdom but a follower of Christ who comes to him who is the fount and source of all love, who comes to be filled with that love and thereby to mediate it. We do, truly, mediate the fruit of our meditation.

Meditation is above all the prayer of simplicity. We must therefore, each one of us, learn to be natural and to allow natural processes to unfold themselves in their own time. So we each find our own speed for saying the mantra. Most people say it in rhythm with their breathing. The important thing is to articulate it clearly in the silence of your mind, a silence that is itself deepening and spreading all the time, and to concentrate on it to the exclusion of all other thoughts. Remember: you begin saying it, you then sound it in your heart, and finally you listen to it with total attention.

As to frequency you must say the mantra for the entire time of the meditation to the rhythm you find for yourself. You will be tempted to rest on your oars, to float in some anesthetized netherworld of your own. The way to transcend the temptation is absolute fidelity to the mantra. This is the condition of rooting it in your heart.   — CM 45–46

In meditation, then, we declare our own poverty. We renounce words, thoughts, imagination, and we do so by restricting the mind to the poverty of one word, and thus the process of meditation is simplicity itself. In order to experience its benefits, it is necessary to meditate twice a day and every day, without fail. Twenty minutes is the minimum time for meditation; twenty-five or thirty minutes is about the average time. It is also helpful to meditate regularly in the same place and also at the same time every day because this helps a creative rhythm in our life to grow, with meditation as a kind of pulse-beat sounding the rhythm. But when all is said and done, the most important thing to bear in mind about meditation is to remain faithfully repeating the mantra throughout the time put aside for it, throughout the time of what the *Cloud of Unknowing* called "the time of the work."   — WS 12

We all need to be encouraged to tread the way faithfully day by day as we return to our morning and evening meditation. We don't need to be encouraged in the progress we are making. That would be altogether too self-conscious an approach to prayer and far too egotistical. Yet we need to take heart constantly and to be encouraged by reflecting on what God has accomplished in Jesus. Looked at from his point of view it is his glory that matters. From our perspective (as long as this is separate) it is our faith, not our purpose, that matters. We should, in the great poverty of the mantra, leave even our progress behind. The way of faith is also the way of humility: "Humble yourselves then under God's mighty hand, and he will lift you up in due time."

This faithful humility and humble fidelity is the way of meditation. Every time we sit down to meditate we humbly leave everything behind and make ourselves as fully available as we can to the power of God released in our hearts. We must learn to be awake, to be alert. Not alert only to ourselves, our ideas, fears, and desires, but alert to God. Christian prayer is not only attention to God, but it is also coming to fullness of being in God. This is our invitation, and our invitation is our destiny, given to us in Jesus. Do not be discouraged, then, and do not try to rate yourself. Measuring your progress has no significance whatever. The only significant measure is the infinite power of Christ in your heart.

Meditation is the way of being, being in God, being-in-love. All that is necessary to know is that we are on the pilgrimage and that we are continuing to be faithful. Continuing to say your mantra as best you can, day by day, with growing simplicity and deepening poverty.   — WMF 35

To meditate each one of us must learn to be wholly still, and that is a discipline. When you meditate you should spend a few moments just getting into a comfortable sitting posture. But then all of us at some time during our meditation feel like moving, and by not moving, by staying still, we will undergo what may perhaps be our first lesson in transcending desires and overcoming that fixation that we so often have with ourselves.

So I want you to understand that meditation does involve this real discipline, and the first discipline we probably have to learn is to sit quite still. That is why it is important to take care of the practical details like wearing loose clothing and finding a comfortable chair or cushion to sit on, so that you can be comfortable and so enter fully and generously into the discipline.

Then you close your eyes gently and begin to repeat your word — *Maranatha*. The purpose of repeating the word is to gently lead you away from your own thoughts, your own ideas, your own desire, your own sin, and to lead you into the presence of God, by turning you around, by turning you away from yourself toward God. Say the word gently but deliberately, say the word in a relaxed way but articulate it silently in your mind, *Ma-ra-na-tha*. Gradually, as you continue to meditate, the word will sink down into your heart. And this experience of liberty of spirit is the uniting of mind and heart in God.

As you begin to meditate all sorts of questions will arise in your mind. Is this for me? What does it mean? Should I be doing this? Am I getting anything out of it? And so forth. All these questions you must leave behind. You must transcend all self-questioning, and you must come to your meditation with childlike simplicity. "Unless you become like little children, you cannot enter the Kingdom of Heaven."

So my advice to you is, say your word, be content to say your word and allow the gift to be given by God. Don't demand it. We should come to our meditation with no demands and no expectations, but with just that generosity of spirit that allows us to be as present as we can to ourselves and to God. Meditating is very, very simple. Don't complicate it. As you meditate you should become more and more simple, not more and more complicated. As you know, nothing in this life that is really worth having can be had without a considerable amount of self-transcendence. It is the real loss of self that brings us the joy. And meditating is having the nerve to take attention off yourself and to put it forward, to put it forward on God, to look ahead.

We are used to dwelling in a world with thousands of mirrors seeing ourselves, seeing how others see us, constantly. Meditating is a definitive smashing of all the mirrors. It is looking, not at reflections of things, not at reflections of yourself. It is looking into the reality that is God. And, in that experience, being expanded into infinity. That is liberty of spirit. The liberty is the fruit of the discipline, and so if you want to learn to meditate it is absolutely necessary to meditate every day. Every day of your life, every morning and every evening. There are no shortcuts. There are no crash courses. There is no instant mysticism. It is simply the gentle and gradual change of direction. The change of heart that comes is to stop thinking of yourself and to be open to God, to the wonder of him, to the glory of him, and to the love of him.   — MC 17–18

Meditation is the way par excellence to handle distractions because the purpose of the one word, the mantra, is simply to bring your mind to peace, silence, and concentration. Not to bring it to rest with holy thoughts alone but to transcend what we know as thought altogether. And the mantra serving this end is like a plough that goes through your mind pushing everything else aside — "making the rough places plain." Cassian spoke of its "casting off and rejecting the rich and ample matter of the manner of thoughts." It is because the mind is "light and wandering," as susceptible to thoughts and images as a feather to the slightest breeze, that Cassian enjoins the mantra as the way to transcend distraction and attain stability.

The essence, the art of saying the mantra, is to say it, sound it, listen to it, and just ignore the distractions. Give primacy to the mantra above all else. Gradually, as you persevere in saying the mantra, distractions do become less and less of a reality.

My teacher used to say that the first three aims that you have when you begin to meditate are these: first of all, just to say the mantra for the full period of your meditation. That's your first goal and that might take a year; it might take ten years. The second goal is to say your mantra and be perfectly calm in the face of all distractions that come. And the third preliminary aim is to say the mantra for the full time of your meditation with no distractions.   — CM 45

The mantra itself is a special kind of word. There are, in other circumstances, other special kinds of words: for example, a hypnotist might suggest to a patient to repeat a word, and the immediate aim in repeating the word would be to go into some kind of deep relaxation. The ultimate aim might be something else, say to give up smoking. What is the immediate aim of saying the mantra?

I think the immediate objective is to bring you to silence. This is what most people will experience when they begin to meditate for the first time. Most people find, not everyone, that very early on they do come to a most extraordinary silence and peacefulness. But then as they proceed this gives way to a very distracted state of being, and they begin to feel during this stage, well, this is hard, perhaps meditation is not for me. I have no talent for it, all I seem to get now when I meditate is more and more distractions. But I think that is the crucial moment to persevere. The ultimate aim of meditation is what motivates you then, and that aim is to bring you to a total silence. As I've probably said to you before, it has to be a silence that is entirely unself-conscious. So as soon as you realize, consciously, that you are in this silence, you must begin to say your mantra again immediately. That trains you in the generosity of not trying to possess the fruit of your meditation. It is very difficult for people today to accept this teaching of the mantra because most people in our society go into something so that they can experience the experience. Meditation is different from that. It is an entry into pure experience.

Now the way that the ancient wisdom expressed this is in the saying that "the monk who knows he is praying is not praying. The monk who does not know he is praying is praying." So say your mantra until you come to total silence. You may be in that silence for a split second. You may be in it for a minute; you may be in it for twenty minutes. But as soon as you realize you are in it, start saying the mantra again. And don't try to make that silence happen. I think that's another hazard — that we want to make progress. We want to get some sort of verification that the whole business of saying the mantra for five years is going to be worth it. At that stage, especially, you must resist the temptation to try to possess the fruits of meditation. We must just meditate and say the mantra and when we realize we have stopped saying it, say it again.

But it's those moments of pure silence that are the moments of revelation. I don't often speak of this because it would be disastrous to try to confect that experience. And no one who is seriously listening to the teaching should ever attempt to confect the experience. What you must do is say your mantra and be content to say it. Be humble to say it. Be simple to say it. The gift of prayer, of pure prayer, the gift of pure contemplation, the gift of pure silence is an absolute gift. It is never something that we can, as it were, earn or twist God's arm to get. When it is given, we accept it with joy and then we say our mantra again. I think that's the distinction between the immediate and ultimate aims.   — HC 90–91

Opening Our Hearts

The wonder of the Christian revelation is of the unity of being: the union of Jesus with the Father, of ourselves with Jesus. And so, when in our meditation we turn away from the restless ego of our fears, desires, and concerns and turn instead toward the Other, we truly find ourselves in Jesus and do so at the source of our being, the love of the Father. This pilgrimage demands courage to turn away from self; but there is no discovery, no arrival, unless in Paul Tillich's phrase, we cross the "frontier of our own identity." This is as true for you and me as it is for the whole church today. Until people, either individually or in community, have transferred their center of consciousness from themselves, they have not found themselves. You will see that the *via media,* the middle way of meditation, is no compromise.

Because of this and because the depth of commitment to which we are called is absolute; meditation is, quite literally, the prayer of faith. And if there is one concept we should get clearly in focus, it is the real meaning of faith. I have spoken before about the fundamental importance of our personal response to the summons of Jesus, of our turning with a whole and un-fragmented consciousness toward the mystery of his indwelling spirit. I have said that as real and powerful as that presence is in our hearts, and as wonderful as the transformation is that it can effect, it will not impose itself on us by force — because it is Love. It will not break through the doors of our hearts. We must open our hearts to it. The wonderful beauty of prayer is that the opening of the heart is as natural as the opening of a flower. Just as a flower opens and blooms when we let it be, so if we simply are, if we become and remain silent, then our hearts cannot but open: the Spirit cannot but pour through into our whole being. It is this we have been created for. It is what the Spirit has been given to us to bring about.   —LH 56–57

It is important to learn to see meditation as a way of growth, a way of deepening our own commitment to life, and so as a way leading to our own maturity. To see this, it is a most important priority for every one of us to allow our spirit two things: first, the deepest possible contact with the Life Force and then, as a

result of that contact, to allow our spirit space within which to
expand. Now when we listen to that as a theory it sounds like
just so many words. What does it mean for us when we say that
a high priority in every life that would be truly human should
be this contact with the Life Source?

Every great spiritual tradition has known that in profound
stillness the human spirit begins to be aware of its own Source.
In the Hindu tradition, for example, the Upanishads speak of
the spirit of the one who created the universe as dwelling in our
heart. The same spirit is described as the one who in silence is
loving to all. In our own Christian tradition Jesus tells us of the
Spirit who dwells in our hearts and of the Spirit as the Spirit of
love. This interior contact with the Life Source is vital for us,
because without it we can hardly begin to suspect the potential
that our life has for us. The potential is that we should grow,
that we should mature, that we should come to fullness of life,
fullness of love, fullness of wisdom. The knowledge of that potential is of supreme importance for each of us. In other words,
what each of us has to do, and what each of us is invited to do,
is to begin to understand the mystery of our own being as the
mystery of life itself.

In the vision proclaimed by Jesus each one of us is invited
to understand the sacredness of our own being and life. That
is why the second priority is of such great importance: namely,
that we should allow our spirit the space within which to expand. In the tradition of meditation this space for expansion of
spirit is to be found in silence, and meditation is both a way of
silence and a commitment to silence which grows in every part
of our lives. It becomes a silence that we can describe only as
the infinite silence of God, the eternal silence. And, as I am sure
you will find from your own experience, it is in this silence that
we begin to find the humility, the compassion, the understanding that we need for our expansion of spirit. Thoughtful men
and women everywhere in the world today are beginning to see

that spiritual growth, spiritual awareness, is the highest priority for our time. But the question is: How do we do it? How do we enter on this path?

That is where the tradition of meditation is of supreme importance for us, as a tradition of spiritual commitment by men and women down the ages and yet a tradition available for you and for me. The only thing that is necessary is that we enter into it by beginning the practice. The practice is very simple and very obvious. We have to put time by; we have to spend some time each morning and each evening of our life to make ourselves available for this work of making space available in our lives for the expansion of spirit. The deepening of faith and the actual practice of meditation are both very simple. Simply take your word, your mantra, and repeat it.

That simplicity is one of the great problems for men and women of our time. We are so used to complexity that the simplicity of meditation, just being content to say your word, to sound your word in your heart, is a major challenge. That is why, when we meditate together or alone, each of us must try to say our word as faithfully as possible, as continually as possible.

The word I recommend you to say, the Aramaic word *Maranatha,* should be said without moving your lips, that is, said interiorly in your heart, and you should continue to sound it from the beginning to the end of your time of meditation. Meditation is a process of growing, of growing more spiritually aware, and, like all processes of growth, it has its own speed, its own pace. It is an organic process. You have as it were to root the mantra in your heart. Jesus so often spoke of the Word of the gospel taking root in the hearts of men and women, and, he tells us, it has to fall into receptive soil. In other words, the whole of your being has to be involved in the process. You sound the mantra, and by your fidelity in returning to it day after day, you root it in your heart, and, once rooted, it flourishes. Indeed it flowers. And the flower of meditation is peace, a profound peace. It is a peace that arises from harmony, from the dynamic harmony that you encounter when you make contact with the ground of your being, because what you discover is that the mantra is rooted in your heart, the center of your being, and your being is rooted in God, the center of all being.

The way of meditation is a way of great simplicity, and so you must take it a day at a time. You don't demand results. You don't look for progress. You simply repeat your mantra every morning and every evening for the entire time of your meditation, and in the process itself, which is a process of forgetting yourself, of taking the searchlight of consciousness off yourself, you find yourself in God. Finding yourself in God, you come to an understanding, which is the understanding of the Is-ness of life. You come to see that your life is a gift, that you offer back to God, and the gift that was a finite gift when it was given to you becomes in the offering back an infinite gift.

Reflect on this in the light of these words from the letter to the Hebrews: "The kingdom we are given is unshakeable; let us therefore give thanks to God, and so worship him as he would be worshiped, with reverence and awe." The awesomeness of God's closeness to us leads us into profound reverence. We have only to learn to be still, to be silent.   —MC 76–78

Just as the Eucharist is both a commemoration and an actual present event, so the mantra spans levels of consciousness and dimensions of time. It is, in a sense, our echoing response to the love-cry of the Spirit, to the whole life of Jesus returning to the Father, a response not at any level of conceptual reasoning but an absolute and unconditional response. Insofar as we are aware of it, it is a response at the deepest level of our being where we acknowledge and experience our complete poverty and complete dependence upon the sustaining love of God. Our response achieves this absolute value, travels to this source level of our being to the extent that we say the mantra with complete simplicity and persevere in our renunciation, at the time of our meditation, of our thoughts, imaginations, of our very self-consciousness. As the mantra becomes rooted more deeply and thoroughly integrated with our consciousness, so does our whole being participate in our response to the Spirit. Its purpose is the integration of all our levels of being with the source of our being, the source that calls the whole person back to itself, awakened through the Spirit of Jesus.   —WS 39–40

The purpose of saying the mantra is that it becomes the focus of your attention. We are not thinking of anything nor are we pursuing any insights that may come to us as we say the mantra. Let them all fall away as you come to an ever deeper silence in which the only sound in your mind is the mantra. The mantra itself will teach you the patience needed to say it. It will also teach you the humility needed. In meditating we are not seeking to possess God or to arrive at a profound insight about God. We are seeking simply to accept the gift of our own creation as fully as we presently can and to respond to it as generously as we can. To do this we learn to be still, to be silent, and to be truly humble.

In commonday language, the essence of meditation is to leave the ego behind. We are not trying to see with the ego what is happening. Ego-vision is limited by its own self-centerlines. The eye with which we see without limit is the eye that cannot see itself. The paradox of meditation is that once we give up trying to see and to possess, then we see all and all things are ours.
                —WMF 8

If we can see prayer in this context we are, I think, on the way to transcending our obstructive self-consciousness about it, about forms or techniques. One must be especially careful, when one comes to consider the form of prayer I have been describing, of not getting sidetracked by thinking about the technique. There could hardly be anything more simple than taking a single word like "Jesus" or "Abba." But sometimes when people hear about meditation for the first time, they miss the simplicity which is the essence and become fixated on what they see as some kind of esoteric, foreign prayer technique. When we're trying to teach this to lay people in Europe or America we find they often get confused when they hear of it for the first time, and the message we find most difficult to convey — the only message there is to convey — is that there is no need for confusion because all is simplicity itself.

We had a dear Irish lady come to one of our groups a few months ago, and I explained to them briefly what had to be done. And I told them that the mantra that I recommend is *Maranatha*. I recommend it because it is Aramaic, the language Jesus himself spoke, because it's probably the most ancient prayer in the church: St. Paul ends Corinthians with it, John ends Revelation with it, it can be found in the Didache — and so forth. Throughout the *Cloud of Unknowing* the author urges us to choose a word that is full of meaning; but that once you have chosen it, to turn from the meaning, and associations and to listen to it as a sound. *Maranatha* is a perfect mantra from that point of view. Anyway, this good lady listened to all this, and then we went into meditation. And when we came out she said, "Oh, Father, a dreadful thing happened once I got into the meditation room. Didn't I forget the mantra!" And she said: I sat there and I thought, how can I meditate if I hadn't the mantra? But, Father, God is good; didn't I remember it after a few minutes: "Macooshla, Macooshla!"

So the mantra is a very, very simple device that is meant to bring you in all simplicity into the presence of the Lord.

— CM 38–39

This is where the mantra is a device of such importance. As we learn to root it in our consciousness, the mantra becomes like a key that opens the door to the secret chamber of our heart. At first, in the set times of our meditation, both morning and evening, saying the mantra is work. We have to learn to become thoroughly familiar with it. But as we progress, as we begin to sound it and to listen to it, then, each and every time we recite it, we enter into and remain in our heart. Thus, by merely calling the mantra to mind at other times of the day, we enter straightaway into the presence of the Creator who dwells within us. "I am with you always," says the Lord.   — WS 22

In the experience of meditation we discover a growing awareness of unity. The mantra, as I have said before, is like a harmonic that sounds within and brings us into a harmonious unity with the whole of creation, within and without. It is like — I am talking poetically — the harmonic of God bringing us into harmony and union with God himself. This experience of unity inspired St. Paul's vision of the cosmic Christ filling the whole universe and leaving no part of it untouched by his redemptive love. "In him everything in heaven and on earth was created, not only things visible but also the invisible orders.... The whole universe has been created through him and for him."

Through the experience of meditation we come to understand that each of us, meaning every living human being, is in a creative relationship with God through Christ. Meditation has such great importance because as each of us comes closer to Christ the whole fabric of human consciousness is knit more closely together. When we come to see this as individuals we also come to realize that the development of our own personal consciousness and the deepening our own spiritual journey is not just a personal matter. It partakes of a responsibility for the whole human race. Meditation teaches us something more: that the more deeply we enter into this mystery of unity the more truly human and humane we become. By deepening our commitment to our own human journey each of us is also deepening our commitment to that part of humanity that we encounter in our daily round.

This is to say our commitment is to the universal Christ. Even more, if that is possible, it is a commitment to the whole creation. This means a committed concern and compassion for the beauty of nature, and of the human spirit expressed in art, a respect for the environment and all it encapsulates in terms of value and beauty. Every part of life is deepened as we enter the mystery of the universal Christ. The longer we meditate the more we see that this vision is one of infinite depth and boundless proportion. But we should never allow the wonder of this vision to blind us to the need for daily fidelity and daily humility.

I was talking to someone who asked if there wasn't a real danger that, if you were to open to this cosmic vision of St. Paul, you would become a really arrogant person, who thought you knew it all, with all the answers and a cold detachment from the needs or sufferings of others. The answer to that, I think, is that anyone who has tried to say their mantra with daily and deepening fidelity has every reason to grow in humility.

Meditation in this sense is a total ascesis. And ascesis is the antidote for arrogance. It is a path to ground you more and more in the strength, the "virtue" of Christ. You thus become aware that that strength comes from beyond yourself, is greater than you and contains you. Yet it is your strength. This is the mystery of the experience of prayer, that the power released in your heart is your power because it is the power of God. Learning to say the mantra is learning to receive everything from God but to receive it fully, not passively or half-heartedly. We respond in meditation with our whole being to the gift of our whole creation. Prayer realizes this inherent potential for expanding in spirit, in union.

As always, we return to the mantra because to see the vision we must become still. To come into contact with God's Spirit in your heart you must come into contact with your own spirit in the simplicity of utter stillness. That is why we must go beyond all analysis, all division and observation and move into unity. And then we move from unity to union.

I don't think we need to be bothered about becoming arrogant. We need only be bothered about fidelity — fidelity to the daily return to meditation and during meditation to the mantra. However often we are taught this, we realize it only in the practice of meditation. It was the one teaching my own teacher gave me. And now, thirty years down the road, I realize it is a teaching of the most extraordinary wisdom.   — WMF 16–18

Simplicity

The greatest temptation of all is to complicate ourselves. "Unless you become like little children...." Meditation simplifies us, simplifies us to the point where we can receive the fullness of truth and the fullness of love. It prepares us and enables us to listen with childlike attention to the Spirit of Jesus within us. As we persevere in meditation, we enter ever more deeply into relationship with the Spirit, with God who is love dwelling in our hearts, enlightening us and vitalizing us.   — WS 18

The way remains one of absolute simplicity. There is no advanced technique involved or complicated books that you need to read. The most simple person can undertake this journey. Indeed, the simpler the better to begin with. All you need for the journey is discipline, commitment to the daily return to it and to making that space in your day and in your heart. And you need faith. The basic faith you need is that you are, that you are valuable, and that you are valued. This is the faith that you are loveable and that you are loved. You need this faith when you

begin, and as you continue on the pilgrimage your faith will
grow, your fears will fall away. The maturing of faith and the
falling away of fear depend on your commitment to the mantra,
which is another way of saying your determination to leave self
behind and to journey into the mystery.   — WU 75

We all know of people who have had visions. I do not at all
doubt their sincerity. But my own conviction, in the teaching of
the tradition, is that the greatest enemy of *oratio pura* — simple
prayer as our participation in Christ's experience of God — is
our imagination. I have tried to find ways of putting this more
palatably to people who are shocked or offended by what seems
to them an insult to their humanity. But I do believe, and believe
it is the belief of the tradition (experience and tradition being
one again), that the more we "think" about God, picture him,
or stir up our imagination for autonomous visions of him, the
less we can experience him. This is not to denigrate theology,
philosophy, or art. But these three fruits of our minds and hearts
have value for ultimate meaning only so far as they clarify, encourage, or purify our journey to the frontiers of the limited
human consciousness. On this frontier we are met by a guide,
who is unlimited consciousness, the person of Jesus Christ. We
reach this frontier only if we travel light, if we have left all behind us, and if we embrace the one who meets us with absolute
trust. At that moment we know from our own experience that
he is the Way, the Truth, and the Life.   — LH 108

4

Letting Go

☩

Meditation, always John Main's theological lens, is the process of self-discovery. The Christian mystical tradition, like the wisdom of the Orient, says that self-knowledge precedes the knowledge of God. The connection between them is found in the process of self-transcendence that brings us to self-knowledge. This self-discovery comes at a price: the death of egotism. The true self shines forth in consciousness only when false ideas and images of the self have been discarded. The pain of renunciation will be in proportion to the degree that we have taken our illusions to be real. To attain the selfhood that is "fullness of life" we must concentrate our whole self away from ideas about ourselves. Self-analysis is neither self-knowledge nor even the way to self-knowledge. It can yield only very limited truths about the self. Self-knowledge results from turning wholly away from self-fixation.

Whereas self-centeredness breeds anxiety and constant insecurity, self-knowledge brings peace. This is a spiritual fruit far deeper than the ideal of mere relaxation with which a materialistic society views the techniques of religion or spirituality. Joy is the other sign of genuine self-knowledge. The joy of self-discovery results from becoming more aware of our

*unbounded potential. Self-knowledge is also characterized by
liberty of spirit because it frees us from the prison of egotistical self-centeredness. Really to know ourselves means to know
we are free from the need to justify or excuse ourselves. We are
free for God, as fullness of being, free from desire, free to be
ourselves.*

*The ambiguities of language can make all this sound rather
narcissistic. John Main explains, however, how altruistic it actually is. We come to self-knowledge by turning from self to the
other. Even more, self-discovery requires the experience of being loved. The monastery, the church, the family, and society
as a whole are contexts in which we are meant to be convinced that we are loved and thereby gain the confidence to
leave self behind. They are places of healing, not perfection. Despite disappointments and evidence to the contrary John Main
had irrepressible faith in the possibility of a human community
of love that drew each of its members out into the full flower
of their identity and potential. To know one's self is to discover
the true self in another, and to know the ultimate Other, God.*

FINDING OUR TRUE SELF

A Christian possesses power, the power of the Risen Lord,
and it is power that consists in the liberation of spirit that is
achieved through the cycle of death and resurrection, through
our participation in the dying and rising of Jesus. What dies
as we persevere in opening ourselves to the Spirit is our narrow, limited ego and all the petty concerns and ambitions with
which it boards over the shaft of our being; what dies is the
fear we experience as we see the light emerging from this shaft;
what dies is everything that obscures us from realizing life, life
in all its fullness. This discovery of our own spirit, our real self,
is an experience that consists of an indescribable joy, the joy

of liberation. But the loss of self which makes it possible, the erosion and the shedding of long familiar illusions require those qualities which have so important a place in St. Paul's teaching: boldness, courage, faith, commitment, and perseverance. It is these qualities, mundane rather than heroic, which enable us to persevere in the daily commitment to the pilgrimage, the fidelity to the twice-daily meditation and the "grand poverty" to which the mantra leads us. These are not home-grown qualities; they are given to us by love, gifts from the Spirit to lead us to himself, to deeper love. There is no way to truth or to the Spirit that is not the way of love. God is love.   —WS 27

There is the leap of faith from ourselves to the Other — and it is the risk involved in all loving. Now only a little experience of the practice of meditation reveals for you that the process of self-impoverishment is a continuous and continually more radical experience. And this is a delicate moment in our development of prayer. For when we begin to realize the totality of the commitment involved in deep, self-surrendering prayer, there is a strong temptation to turn back, to evade the call to total poverty, to give up meditation, to give up the ascesis of the mantra and to return to self-centered rather than God-centered prayer.

The temptation is to return to that prayer we might describe as the prayer of anesthetized, floating piety — the prayer that John Cassian termed the *pax perniciosa* (the ruinous peace) and the *sopor letalis* (the lethal sleep). This is a temptation we have to transcend. Jesus has called us to lose our life; not to lend it, not to hold out negotiations for better terms. If we lose it, and only if we lose it, will we find it in him. And the vision of prayer of John Cassian, restricting our mind to one word, is proof of the genuineness of our renunciation. In his vision of prayer we renounce thought, imagination, even self-consciousness itself — the matrix of language and reflection.

But let us be quite clear why we renounce all these gifts of God at the time of prayer, at what the author of the *Cloud* calls "the time of the work." It would not be enough to say that we renounce them merely because they "distract." It would indeed be absurd for us to deny that they are the primary natural means of self-understanding and communication. Nor do we renounce them because we consider that they have no place in either our social or personal relationship with God. It is obvious that the whole of our liturgical response to God is based on word, gesture, and image. And Jesus himself has told us that we can pray to the Father in his name for whatever we need, for the needs of the whole world.

All these considerations must constantly be kept sight of. But at the center of our being I think all of us know the truth of what Jesus means when he invites us to lose our lives so that we may find them. At this same center we, all of us, feel the need for a radical simplicity, a moving beyond all our activities to the unitary principle of activity itself: the cause and end of movement. In other words, we all know the need we have to rejoice in our being at its simplest, where it simply exists with no reason for its existence other than it gives glory to God who created it, who loves it and who sustains it in being. Having surrendered everything we have, everything by which we exist or know that we exist, we stand before the Lord in utter simplicity. And the poverty of the single verse that John Cassian enjoins is the means in meditation of losing our life that we may find it, of becoming nothing that we may become the All.

— CM 33–34

Once our spirit is opened to the Spirit of God, division is over. We do not have to play games any more. We can act consistently from our deepest integrity. Nothing can divide our heart once we are open to the Spirit. We have only to learn generosity of heart to be wholly at the disposition of God in the utter openness of love, without demands or expectations of rewards.

My advice is to see your times of meditation not as times that are at your own disposition at all. See your meditation, your prayer, not as your own but as the prayer of Jesus. As long as we are self-importantly thinking of our meditation, or our prayer, we have not fully started this pilgrimage. The time is his; the prayer is his. The miracle is that his prayer is ours, and the miracle is worked in simplicity bringing us to that total and unshakeable confidence in the Father, which the gospel describes as hope. We approach meditation with hope rather than desire: without hesitation and with a childlike sense of being available to God.

We learn to say the mantra with this same simplicity. We are not analyzing it, or its effects, in a calculating way. We say it with a wholly sincere, self-emptying love. Yet by virtue of this self-emptying we are filled with the power of God and with the knowledge that we are one with God because we are loveable and loved. The only requirement is total selflessness expressed in the total abandoning of all our own thoughts, imaginations, insights, and, above all, our own prayers. This is our openness to the prayer of Jesus in our heart.

The ancient writers called meditation the practice of purity of heart. We have to purify, which means to clarify, our consciousness so that we can see with perfect clarity of vision. What we see is what is there. We see ourselves. We see creation. We see God. In his light we see light.

The revelation of all this is his. We learn from the faithfulness of our daily meditation how to wait on God and to attend to God in the deepening patience of true presence and mindfulness. In a growing fidelity and clarity of consciousness I urge you to put aside all the irrelevant kinds of speculation: am I enjoying this, am I getting anything out of this, am I becoming wiser or holier?

We know that there is a pilgrimage to make. It is a journey away from self and into the mystery of God. It is an amazing grace that each of us can and does know this, or at least suspect it. To know it is really to know everything because we have only to begin and continue. To be on the pilgrimage is everything.

We must learn to become simple, one, whole. We must learn to become peace, so that we become ourselves. In meditation we learn to be and in learning this we learn with unshakeable certainty that God is. When you meditate, sit upright, close your eyes, and say your word, without speculation, without self-consciousness, without haste, simply like a child, until the end of the meditation.   —WMF 14–15

Meditation is the process in which we take time to allow ourselves to become aware of our infinite potential in the context of the Christ-event. As St. Paul puts it in chapter 8 of Romans: "and those whom he called, he has justified, and to those whom he justified, he has also given his splendor."

In meditation we open ourselves up to this splendor. Put another way, this means that in meditation we discover both who we are and why we are. In meditation we are not running away from ourselves, we are finding ourselves; we are not rejecting ourselves, we are affirming ourselves. St. Augustine put this very succinctly and very beautifully when he said: "Man must first be restored to himself that, making in himself as it were a stepping-stone, he may rise thence and be borne up to God."   —WS 4

Meditation summons us to open our hearts to light and life by the very simple expedient of paying attention; that is, paying attention to their presence within us. We pay attention to our own true nature, and by becoming fully conscious of the union of our nature with Christ, we become fully ourselves. By becoming fully ourselves we enter the fullness of life Jesus has brought us. We come to appreciate in the reverent silence of our prayer that we are infinitely holy as temples of God's own Spirit. We learn to remember who we are and that our vocation is to look upon and contemplate the Godhead itself and thus to be ourselves divinized. As the third Eucharistic Prayer expresses it: "On that day we shall see you, our God, as you are, and we shall become like you." The great masters of prayer in the Christian tradition have understood prayer in this way as a discovery of self that takes us far beyond narrow self-consciousness, a discovery made by making of ourselves a stepping-stone. The twelfth-century Scot Richard of St. Victor expresses it so clearly and simply:

> The rational soul finds in itself the chief and principal mirror for seeing God. Let him who desires to see God wipe his mirror and cleanse his heart. When the mirror has been cleansed and examined a long time carefully, a brightness of the divine light begins to shine through to him and a great beam of illumination not known hitherto appears before our eyes.

Saying the mantra is just this process of polishing the mirror, the mirror within us, so that our heart becomes fully open to the work of God's love for us, fully reflecting the light of that love. We must understand very clearly that the first step in this process is to set our own house in order. Meditation is thus a process of self-discovery. By faithfulness to the twice-daily meditation we find that in the Christian tradition self-discovery and self-affirmation are the realization of our own true grandeur and true splendor in Christ. St. Catherine of Genoa put it this way: "My me is God nor do I know my selfhood save in him." In the Indian tradition the same understanding finds expression in the assertion that our first task is the discovery of our own true inner self, the Atman, which is the means of becoming aware of union with the ultimate universal self, which is Brahman, which is God.

Similarly, in the Christian perspective, we see the great task of prayer as the realization of our intimate union with God, our Father, through Christ in the Spirit. St. Gregory wrote of St. Benedict that "he dwelt within himself always in the presence of his Creator and not allowing his eyes to gaze on distractions." There is something extraordinarily attractive about the description. It reveals an understanding of the Father of Western monasticism as above all a man of prayer. "He dwelt within himself." That tells us that in Gregory's view, Benedict had realized a wholeness and harmony that had dispelled all false ideas, all illusions about himself, illusions which are necessarily outside of ourselves.

The task we have is to find our way back to our creative center where wholeness and harmony are realized, to dwell within ourselves, leaving behind all the false images of ourselves such as what we think we are, or what we think we might have been, because these have an unreal existence outside us. Remaining within ourselves, in this sense of illusion-shattering honesty and simplicity, leads us to remain always in the presence of our Creator.   — WS 20–21

Learning to say the mantra is learning to turn aside from that very self-consciousness and self-preoccupation that complicates us and loads us down with the riches that prevent us from becoming conscious of the Spirit within us, alive and active in our inmost centers. The "riches" that the gospel tells us make it so difficult to enter the Kingdom are the limited, incomplete truths that result from our self-analysis. We have to understand with simple clarity that self-analysis is not self-knowledge nor is it even the way to self-knowledge. The little half-truths our self-analysis reveals are merely refractions of the great, single, simple and central truth. To know ourselves we have to turn wholly away from all self-preoccupation and even from those ways in which we are self-conscious. This is the great poverty of Christ centered in the Father who sent him and spoke through him (John 8:28). It is the great poverty, the great richness and generosity of the mantra. No one should ever say this is easy. Nor should anyone say it is impossible for anyone. It demands only faith. To know ourselves means to discover our selves in another. Our ultimate self-knowledge, which is the Spirit of Christ, united to our spirit, means discovering ourselves in God. But to turn from self involves courage because it can seem as if we are turning away from all we have and know toward nothing. "No one can be a follower of mine unless they leave self behind and follow me." Every act of faith is a step into the infinite expanse of God.

Faced with this challenge to Be, people can react by making an image of God from their own self-conscious preoccupations and addressing themselves to this image, talking to it, "listening" to it. People are even advised to talk over their problems with God. Hearing this sort of advice I can only recall the words of Jesus: "In your prayer do not go babbling on like the heathen who imagine the more they say the more likely they are to be heard. Do not imitate them. Your Father knows what your needs are before you ask him. This is how you should pray.... "

Jesus then gave his followers the seven short, rhythmical phrases for their prayer that we know as the Lord's Prayer. Jesus' teaching on prayer emphasizes for us time and again that prayer is always a growth in selflessness, in simplicity, in unity of consciousness with the Spirit.

There is another way we can react to (or rather, evade) this challenge to Be. We can accept that we have to renounce multiplicity of thought and imagination but then just set off wandering in the labyrinthine ways of our psyches, savoring our own experiences, setting our own courses, acting as our own guides. This is to be more turned upon ourselves than ever, more than ever turned away from the inner guide that is the Spirit, whom we find by turning from self-centerlines and from the outer guide that is our Christian tradition. —LH 94–95

Meditation and the poverty of it is no form of self-rejection. We are not running away from ourselves, nor do we hate ourselves. On the contrary, our search is a search for ourselves and the experience of our own personal and infinite capacity to be loved. The harmony of the real Self that lies beyond all selfishness, beyond all ego-based activity is so well attested to in the Christian tradition. St. Catherine of Genoa put it succinctly: "My me is God. Nor do I know my selfhood save in him." But to arrive at our selfhood — and it is to that invitation we respond when we meditate — or, putting it in the more felicitous and perhaps more accurate language of the East, to realize ourselves, we must pass into the radical experience of personal poverty with an unflinching self-surrender.

And what we surrender, what we die to is, in the thought of Zen, not the self or the mind but rather that image of the self or the mind which we have mistakenly come to identify with who we really are. Now this is not a proposition that we need, as the *Cloud of Unknowing* says, "to expound with imaginative cleverness." But it does indicate that what we are renouncing in prayer is, essentially, unreality. And the pain of the renunciation will be in proportion to the extent that we took our illusions to be real. In prayer we divest ourselves of the illusion of the isolating ego: we do so in a sustained act of faith by concentrating our entire self away from the idea of ourselves, by concentrating on the real Self, created in God, redeemed by Jesus, a temple of the Holy Spirit.

We must first come near to ourselves by finding our own true Self. But we have still to learn to enter into the paradox that Jesus has put before us: "The person who would find his life [*psyche*] must first lose it." Meditation is the prayer of faith because we are willing to follow the teacher's command: we are willing to lose our lives so that we may realize fully our own potential.

And when we have found our true Self, our task is, as it were, only beginning. For as soon as we have found ourselves, what we have done — again in St. Augustine's expression — is to have found the essential "stepping-stone" that will lead us to God. Because then — and only then — do we find the confidence necessary to take the next step, which is to stop looking at our newfound Self, to turn the searching off ourselves and onto the Other. And meditation is the prayer of Faith precisely because we leave ourselves behind before the Other appears, and with no prepackaged guarantee that he will appear. The essence of all poverty consists in this risk of annihilation.   — CM 32–33

The two dangers you must avoid are, first of all, distraction, not allowing your mind to become involved in trivia. The second is that you must not allow yourself to be just nowhere. Prayer is not just floating in space. It is a full and fully conscious entry into the prayer of Jesus. It is in fact having his mind. As St. Paul says, "We possess the mind of Christ." One of the constantly recurring themes of the Buddhist scriptures is the warning to humanity not to waste life, not to allow life to slip through our fingers until we suddenly become aware that it is all over. Your life is for living. Your life is for coming into full consciousness, full enlightenment. In the teaching of St. Paul, we are allowing the light of Christ to shine with its full brilliance in our heart. The underlying rationale of the Buddhist scriptures is that we must be serious about the purpose of life and not trivialize it or allow it to pass away in an endless series of distractions. As Christians we must be utterly serious about the gift that has been given us: the gift of life and the gift of redemption. By this we are made one with God in Jesus, and as Christians we should be proclaiming this gospel to the whole world, saying that each of us is made for this destiny of oneness in fullness of life. That is the essence of the Christian proclamation. We must understand that this is now accomplished in Jesus, if only we will realize it. Meditation is our acceptance of the gift, the gift

of life, the gift of Jesus and the self-giving of his Spirit. Because
the gift is infinite, it requires our full attention and complete
concentration. We are not spending half an hour in the morning
and half an hour in the evening going in for a "bit of religion"
or doing spirituality as part of our health program. In these
half-hours we seek to live the eternal moment. We seek to set
aside everything that is passing away and to live in the eternity
of God.   —WU 63–64

Freedom of Spirit

One of the things that I suppose everybody strives for in their
life is to discover a real liberty of spirit. We are constrained by
so many things — by fear and by trying to project the image of
ourselves that we feel others expect. I think people suffer a great
deal of frustration because they cannot be themselves and cannot make contact with themselves. James Joyce once described
one of his characters as "always living at a certain distance from
himself." Now what Jesus came to proclaim was precisely this
liberty. The liberty to be ourselves and the liberty to find ourselves in him, through him, and with him. Meditation is simply
the way to that liberty. It is the way to your own heart. It is
the way to the depth of your own being where you can simply
be — not having to justify yourself or apologize for yourself but
simply rejoicing in the gift of your being. Freedom is not just
freedom from things. Christian liberty is not just freedom from
desire, from sin. We are free for intimate union with God, which
is another way of saying we are free for infinite expansion of
Spirit in God.

Meditation is entering into that experience of being free for
God, transcending desire, sin, leaving it behind; transcending
ego, leaving it behind, so that the whole of our being is utterly available to God. It is in that profound availability that
we become ourselves.   —MC 16

One of the most difficult things for Westerners to understand is that meditation is not about trying to make anything happen. But all of us are so tied into the mentality of techniques and production that we inevitably first think that we are trying to engineer an event, a happening. According to our imagination or predispositions, we may have different ideas of what would happen. For some it is visions, voices, or flashes of light. For others, deep insights and understanding. For others again, better control over their daily lives and problems. The first thing to understand, however, is that meditation has nothing to do with making anything happen. The basic aim of meditation is indeed quite the contrary, simply to learn to become fully aware of what is. The great challenge of meditation is to learn directly from the reality that sustains us.

The first step toward this — and we are invited to take it — is to come into contact with our own spirit. Perhaps the greatest tragedy of all is that we should complete our life without ever having made full contact with our own spirit. This contact means discovering the harmony of our being, our potential for growth, our wholeness — everything that the New Testament, and Jesus himself, called "fullness of life."

So often we live our life at 5 percent of our full potential. But of course there is no measure to our potential; the Christian tradition tells us it is infinite. If only we will turn from self to other, our expansion of spirit becomes boundless. It is all-turning: what the New Testament calls conversion. We are invited to unlock the shackles of limitation, to be freed from being prisoners within our self-limiting egos. Conversion is just this liberation and expansion arising when we turn from ourselves to the infinite God. It is also learning to love God, just as in turning to God we learn to love one another. In loving we are enriched beyond measure. We learn to live out of the infinite riches of God.   —WMF 19–20

STAGES OF THE JOURNEY

Everything John Main teaches about the nature of meditation is validated in the advice he gives about the journey itself. Each time we sit down to meditate we start from scratch, abandoning everything each time, accumulating nothing. This does not mean there is no progress but that the best way to make progress is not to be concerned about it, to put the very desire to succeed and advance into what we abandon. This is easier said than done. But it does help to be reminded that we do not need to evaluate each meditation and that the only measure is to be found in the experience of the infinite. It is only necessary to know you are on the pilgrimage. The fruits of meditation — such as growing fearlessness and peace, compassion and sensitivity — are then recognized not as egotistically satisfying achievements but as the expansion of the divine life in us.

Meditation is a way we tread within the greater Way that is Christ himself. In his lifetime he followed his own journey, his destiny in Jerusalem, but now in the Spirit he has himself become the Way. The way of meditation followed in a supportive Christian community develops our awareness of this greater, inclusive Way. We come to know Jesus as we meditate day by day.

Shortly before his death in December of 1982, John Main composed the last of his newsletters, included here in full as the last part of this section. It was a contemplation of death at the feast of the birth of Jesus, and this paradox allowed him to reflect on the whole journey of life. End and beginning, he says, are two ends of the string of life held in the mystery of God and joined together in the mystery of Christ. Progress on this journey is not measured by achieving a sequence of milestones. We are always learning, always preparing, and we are always being led back to the starting point of all being, which is the love that is God. As this experience of love deepens our commitment to

the spiritual meaning of our lives, Christ is formed in us by faith
and he grows to fullness in us.

On Pilgrimage

The stages of our progress in meditation will come about in
their own time. God's own time. We in fact only hinder this
progression by becoming too self-conscious about our stage of
development. This is where a teacher is of immense help for
keeping you on a straight course. But basically your teacher has
only one instruction to give you and that is: to say your mantra.
More than this is simply encouragement and comfort until the
mantra is rooted in your consciousness. The path of enlightenment is one we tread for ourselves. Each person wins wisdom
for himself or herself. The teacher is there to keep you steadily
going forward. The word "guru" itself, dispeller of darkness,
means the one who is steady.   — WS 17–18

The metaphor of a pilgrimage is one that often occurs to us as
we reflect on our life. It well describes the roundabout way that
Augustine Baker found his entry into the tradition of Christian
prayer, no less than it describes the physical undertaking of Cassian and Germanus in their journey to the Egyptian desert. But
each and every one of us is called to follow this same pilgrimage
to uncover the prayer of Jesus in our heart.

All that I have said to you this evening is what I have been
able to discover in my own limited experience. I am not suggesting for a moment that this is the only way there is to pray. There
are, of course, many mansions in the Father's Kingdom. But it
is the only way I have been able to discover, and it is a way of
great simplicity. All you have to do is to find your word, ideally
with the help of a teacher, and then faithfully to repeat it. But
don't let me mislead you. Actually to say the word morning and
evening, day in and day out, winter and summer, whether you

feel like it or don't feel like it, all this requires a good deal of grit and steel in the spine. Remember Serapion. But if you can say it, I think it will bring you to an understanding of your monastic life that will bring it incredible richness.   — CM 21–22

The way we set out on this pilgrimage of "other-centerlines" is to recite a short phrase, a word that is commonly called today a mantra. The mantra is simply a means of turning our attention beyond ourselves — a way of unhooking us from our own thoughts and concerns.

Reciting the mantra brings us to stillness and to peace. We recite it for as long as we need to before we are caught up into the one prayer of Jesus. The general rule is that we must first learn to say it for the entire period of our meditation each morning and each evening and then to allow it to do its work of calming over a period of years.

The day will come when the mantra ceases to sound and we are lost in the eternal silence of God. The rule when this happens is not to try to possess this silence, to use it for one's own satisfaction. The clear rule is that as soon as we consciously realize that we are in this state of profound silence and begin to reflect about it we must gently and quietly return to our mantra.

Gradually the silences become longer and we are simply absorbed in the mystery of God. The important thing is to have the courage and generosity to return to the mantra as soon as we become self-conscious of the silence.

It is important not to try to invent or anticipate any of the experiences. I hope that it will become clear that each of us is summoned to the heights of Christian prayer — each of us is summoned to fullness of life. What we need however is the humility to tread the way very faithfully over a period of years so that the prayer of Christ may indeed be the grounding experience of our life.   — MC xi–xii

The pilgrimage of prayer is followed between two dead ends of illusion: "talking your problems over" is always likely to lead you deeper into ego fixation, and "drifting in an undisciplined self-observation" is likely to isolate you more effectively from God, from others, and from yourself. This is why the simplicity and the poverty of the mantra are so vital to the pilgrimage of meditation. In saying it with fidelity we are doing all we are called to do, which is to turn from self. The rest we leave to the free gift of God, without desire or expectation. We begin in faith. We continue in faith. In faith we arrive. Our opportunity and our responsibility is to be self-emptying disciples of our Master. A disciple is not greater than his master. It is enough that we should become like him. Our way to imitate his whole-hearted kenosis, his self-emptying, is the way of prayer. It is a real journey we are on, with real demands and a real realization. And so we must really be faithful to our word: not just thinking of saying it but saying it with simplicity and love.

The reality of God is like a sea. Isolated from reality, we are like people standing on the shore. Some sit, like King Canute, ordering the tide to turn back. Others gaze romantically at its beauty and vastness from a safe distance. But we are called to be baptized, to be plunged into it, to allow its all-powerful tide to direct our lives. To do this we have to leave our familiar dry shore and travel to the further shore of our origin. The poverty and joy of our word leads us into the sea and, once there, it keeps us simply in the current of the Spirit that leads us to a place unknown to us, where we know ourselves in him, in his eternal now. —LH 95–96

We can so easily diffuse the power of God. We can make our religion just the fulfilling of external rites, sacrifices, rules where the heart, the knowledge of God, is asleep. And when you come to consider it, what can be a greater shattering of our own complacency than the knowledge of God? If we could really know

who God is, if we could really have that experience of the reality of his presence, then our own lack of religious commitment
would be exposed and we would be utterly shattered. Turning
to the Lord — the knowledge of God — brings with it a profound silence. Once we have encountered the Spirit of the living
God, the only authentic response possible is a profound and
reverential silence.

The thing we have to face with the challenge of conversion
is that we do have to be changed. We like to think that we are
going to change ourselves in our own time and at our own pace.
But the essence of conversion is that in turning to the Lord he
changes us. I suppose the reality with most of us is that we are
not too keen on being changed. We much prefer to run the show
at our own pace. We like to call the shots and have things under
our control. The essence of conversion is that the Lord God is
going to call the shots, and we are going to be changed, as he
wants us to be changed. As you continue to say the mantra,
and as you deepen your silence in prayer, do not be surprised
if you find in yourself some strong reservations about it, even
some annoyance about it, possibly some anger about it. What
dawns on us as we experience more fully the poverty of it is that
it is now quite literally the Lord's prayer, not mine any longer.
We have given up our own words; we have given up our own
monologues; we have given up our own recitations. Now it is
the Lord's prayer because we respond at his pleasure. Once that
begins to dawn on us, we can get quite restless because most
of us, if we are honest, do not really want to be changed. We
want to have our religion under our control just the same way
that we want to have most other things and most other people
under our own control.   — AW 22–23

To awaken is to open our eyes, and we open them, as St. Benedict said, "to the divinizing light." What we see transforms
what we are.

Each time we meditate we take a step further into this wake-fulness, this state of being in light. And the more fully we integrate the basic Christian experience into our ordinary daily life the more deeply wakeful we become. This makes our life a journey of discovery, an exploration, a constantly renewed miracle of created vitality. To meditate is to put an end to dull-ness, to fear, and above all to pettiness. What is vital is that we are really on this journey, not just thinking about the journey or talking about it. A peculiar danger for religious people is to believe that because they are so religious they have all the an-swers taped. The frightful arrogance of the religious egoist is to believe that he has arrived before he has even started. It is easy to read about wakefulness, to have elaborate and, as far as they go, accurate ideas about enlightenment, and yet all the while be fast asleep. The man who is awake knows without doubt that he is awake. But the man who is dreaming also believes that he is awake. In that state, the images of a dream convince us that they are the realities we know as real when we are awake. We enter wakefulness, as the meditator knows, by letting go of the images and by learning to wait for the Reality — for "Christ to shine upon you."

This is the basic Christian experience I was speaking of. It is perennial, unchanging, but also it is new in every generation and unique for every individual and unique every time we medi-tate. Every time we meditate we enter into the vitalizing creative presence of God. It is its manifold uniqueness that gives us our common ground, our oneness in him. This is the basis of all Christian community. The dynamic of the experience is always conversion, a turning from self to the Other, a rediscovery of a realm beyond ourselves and yet in which we have our own real and unique place. The dream image we let go of is of a universe revolving around us as its center. The reality revealed — and the burden of illusion lifted — is the revelation that we are in our own unique and indispensable place in the universe, a universe that is centered in God and that is permeated by his presence, for his center is everywhere.   — PC 73–74

More and more people who have been meditating for some years are now awakening to the community of silent love they share. I want to remind you again of the importance of the discipline involved. The journey is away from all egoism. In the words of Jesus, "No one can be a follower of mine, unless they leave self behind." It is surprising to discover that the first step in self-transcendence is to be still. In meditation this asks us to learn the discipline of sitting still. In that stillness the body becomes an outward sign of the inward stillness that you approach in your pilgrimage of the mantra. Even as you become a committed meditator, do not underestimate the importance of an upright alert posture and of absolute stillness. Both contribute to the preparation for that inward stillness wherein the mystery unfolds itself. The journey of meditation is a journey into the mystery of being. It is a journey in which we discover our own mystery as part of the infinite mystery.   — WU 74–75

The Oceans of God

At Christmas we become more sharply aware of the mysterious blend of the ordinary and the sublime in the monastic life and indeed in all life that is really Christian. It is important, though, to see it as a blend, not as an opposition.

It is tempting to treat the birth of Christ as something romantically outside the full meaning of his life, something pre-Christian. In the rich and beautiful gospel accounts of his birth we can be tempted to see this part of his life as merely consoling or idyllic. But it is part of the human mystery that nothing is outside the Mystery. By the incarnation God accepted this aspect of the human condition, and so the birth and childhood of Christ are part of the mystery of his life — a life that culminated on the cross and reached its transcendent completion in the resurrection and ascension.

Our meditation teaches us how fully every part of us has to be involved in the radical conversion of our life. It teaches us that we have to put our whole heart into this work of the Spirit if we are genuinely to respond to the call to leave the shallows and enter into the deep, direct knowledge that marks a life lived in the mystery of God. Then everything in our life acquires this depth dimension of divine Presence. We are foolish to look for "signs" on the way — it is a form of spiritual materialism that Jesus rebuked — because if we are on the way, which means in the Mystery, in the bright cloud of God's presence, then all things are signs. Everything mediates the love of God.

There is of course, literary art in the infancy narratives of Luke and Matthew. But this does not mean that the details of the birth of Christ were not charged with wonder and mystery for those who were involved in it. The parents of Jesus "wondered" at what was being said about him. And Mary teaches us how this experience of wonder is to be assimilated by "treasuring these things in her heart." The "heart" is that focal point in our being where we can simply be in the Mystery without trying to explain or dissect it. A mystery analyzed becomes merely another problem. It must be apprehended whole and entire. And that is why we, who are called to apprehend it, must ourselves be made one in mind and heart.

The mystery surrounding Jesus was perceptible from the beginning of his life. Not until his death and resurrection was it capable of being fully apprehended, fully known. Because not until then was it complete. Our life does not achieve full unity until it transcends itself and all limitations by passing through death. This is why we do not fully comprehend the mystery of Christ, in which we enter the mystery of God, until our life is complete. We begin to enter it as soon as our consciousness begins to stir into vital perception and to learn the laws of reality by learning to love and be loved. But we are always learning, always preparing for the fullness that comes to us all. Until the life of Jesus passed through death and returned in the resurrection this completion was a source of terror or despair to the human race. Now it has been transformed. For what seemed a dead-end has now been revealed to the eyes of faith as a bridge. This is the hidden significance of the birth of Jesus, his growth through infancy and manhood, and his supreme sacrifice of self on the cross. In our beginning is our end. And so in the birth of Jesus death already began to be transformed. All the intuitions shared by those involved in his birth and his early life were fulfilled in his ministry and the paschal mystery. His life, like every human life, has a hidden and mysterious unity. End and beginning are two ends of the string of life held in the mystery of God and joined together in the mystery of Christ.

Our life is a unity because it is centered in the mystery of God. But to know its unity we have to see beyond ourselves and with a perspective greater than we generally see with when self-interest is our dominant concern. Only when we have begun to turn from self-interest and self-consciousness does this larger perspective begin to open.

Another way of saying that our vision expands is to say that we come to see beyond mere appearances, into the depth and significance of things. Not just the depth and significance in relation to ourselves is involved but depth in relation to the whole of which we are part. This is the way of true self-knowledge, and it is why true self-knowledge is identical with true humility. Meditation opens up for us this precious form of knowledge, and it is what enables us to pass beyond mere objectivity — merely looking at the mystery of God as observers — and to enter the mystery itself. This knowledge becomes wisdom once we have entered the cloud of the mystery and when we know no longer by analysis and definition but by participation in the life and spirit of Christ.

So we learn by the path of meditation what cannot be learned otherwise, what is unknowable as long as we hesitate to become pilgrims of the Spirit. Following this path is a fundamental requirement of the Christian life, which must be a life lived out of the depths rather than the shallows. This is why Christian discipleship is the completion of the human condition. In this condition man always seeks the complete action, something that will call forth all his powers simultaneously, focus and unify all the dimensions of his being. Until we have found this action we are restless, always mastered by distraction or desire masquerading as the reality which only this perfect action can lead us into.

Naturally, if we are truly human we know that this action is love. Only when we live in and out of love do we know that miraculous harmony and integration of our whole being which makes us fully human. This is always a practical rather than idyllic state: I mean that the human condition is always made up of frailties and imperfections, either of personality or environment. The incarnation of God in the human condition, however, absorbs all these faults and accidents in such a way that they can no longer prevent us from the fullness of love. The saint is not superhuman but fully human.

Every part of us, including our faults and failures, must be included in our commitment to the pilgrimage into this fullness. Nothing real is excluded from the kingdom of heaven. Realistic, human wholeness is the cumulative experience of staying on our pilgrimage. Gradually the separate compartments of our life coalesce. The room dividers are taken down and we find that our heart is not a person made up of a thousand individual cells but a great chamber filled with the light of God whose walls are constantly being pushed back.

Meditation expands our knowledge of God because, in leading us into self-knowledge, it propels us beyond self-consciousness. We know God to the degree that we forget ourselves. This is the paradox and the risk of prayer. It is not enough to study the paradox because, like love, it can be known only when it is lived firsthand. Once we have begun to live it we can read the great human testimonies of the spirit — the New Testament and spiritual classics — from within the same experience. Until then, however, we are merely observers, at best waiting to begin.

Can one grasp the spirit? It is not an easy paradox to grasp. How *can* one grasp the spirit? It helps if we reflect on the human manifestations of the essential structure of reality. To love other persons involves more than thinking of them, more even than enjoying their company, more even than sacrificing oneself for them. It involves allowing ourselves to be loved by them. This is perhaps the most moving and awe-inspiring mystery of the incarnation. In becoming human God allows himself to be loved within the human range of love, as ordinarily as any infant, child, adolescent, or adult.

The humility of God in allowing himself to be loved in the man Jesus is our cue for recognizing the basic structure of all reality. Our first step in loving God is to allow ourselves to be loved. The grammar of language is misleading here because there is nothing passive about allowing ourselves to be loved. Just as there is nothing passive about turning our attention off ourselves and nothing passive about saying the mantra — which are the ways we allow ourselves to be loved in any human or divine relationship.

Meditation takes us into the basic relationship of our life. It does so because it leads us into the intimacy with God that arises out of the eternal reality of his loving and knowing us. In doing so he calls us into being, and human being is itself a response to the demand inherent in God's love and knowledge of us. It is the demand that we love and know him. Yet, we can know him, not as an object of our knowledge, but only by participation in his own self-knowledge, his life, and his spirit. Thus we are led back to the starting point of our being, his love and knowledge of us. We come to know and love God because we allow him to know and love us. We allow his self-knowledge to become our self-knowledge. This is the alchemy of love.

Knowledge such as this is certain and unshakeable. "Be rooted and founded in love," wrote St. Paul. Just as the roots of trees hold the soil firm and stop erosion, so it is the roots of love that hold the ground of our being together. They provide the context in which we live and grow. And they each trace back to God as the first root of all being. The roots of love in our life bring us into context with him, with ourselves, and with each other. And they show us that to be is to be in connection, each contributing to the other.

Sanity and balance mean knowing the context in which we live. This form of knowledge makes us sensitive to the presence of God in all our surroundings. Meditation teaches us in the only certain way, by experience, that his presence is not external to us. It is interior, the presence that makes up and holds together the ground of our being. So we come no longer to look for God's presence in the externals of our life but to recognize him in them because our eyes are opened interiorly to his indwelling spirit. We no longer try to grasp hold of God to possess him. Rather we are grasped by his presence, interiorly and exteriorly, because we know that his presence is all pervasive and the ground of all that is.

To be possessed by God in this way is the only true freedom. The tyranny of love is the only true relationship. Inevitably we fear this as it develops or emerges during our pilgrimage, because our image of freedom is so different, so naively imagined as the freedom to do rather than to be. But if we have the courage to be simple and humble enough to enter this real freedom, then we discover in ourselves the power of a faith that is unshakeable. Christian confidence is the discovery of this unshakeability, and it is this confidence that underlies Christian compassion, tolerance, and acceptance. We are made wonderfully secure in our own existence by this discovery, and out of this security we are empowered to drop our defenses and to go out to the other. Our faith is unshakeable, not rigid, because it is one with the ground of our being. Through Christ's union with his disciples his faith becomes their faith, and their faith is not an adjunct to their being. It is the breath of their spirit's life.

So deepening our commitment to this pilgrimage means deepening the knowledge that faith gives birth to it in the soul. As Christ is formed in us, as we ourselves live no longer for ourselves but for him and as his spirit breathes the new life of faith into our mortal bodies, we do come to know Christ more deeply. Maybe it sounds arrogant to say we come to know Christ as we persevere in meditation. But the truth is not less than this. We come to know what it is to live every moment, every decision, every joy or difficulty from within his presence and so out of the infinite resources of his power — the power of love and compassion, an unshakeable reality.

How do we enter this presence? How can we acquire this "knowledge that is beyond knowledge"? Because it is the knowledge of unknowing, it is the presence that forms when we allow ourselves to go beyond being present merely to ourselves and instead become present to God — to be known and loved into full being by him. As we are unformed he is formed. We have to learn to forget ourselves. Nothing is simpler to do. It is the condition of full simplicity. Yet nothing — it seems to me — is more difficult for us. It is so easy in theory to accept this. But in practice it is so difficult to live and love as if the other were really more important than ourselves, or as if our first loyalty were really not to self but to the other.

The greatest difficulty is to begin, to take the first step, to launch out into the depth of the reality of God as revealed in Christ. Once we have left the shore of our own self we soon pick up the currents of reality that give us our direction and momentum. The more still and attentive we are, the more sensitively we respond to these currents. And so the more absolute and truly spiritual our faith becomes. By stillness in the spirit we move in the ocean of God. If we have the courage to push off from the shore we cannot fail to find this direction and energy. The further out we travel the stronger the current becomes, and the deeper our faith. For a while the depth of our faith is challenged by the paradox that the horizon of our destination is always receding. Where are we going with this deeper faith? Then gradually we recognize the meaning of the current that guides us and see that the ocean is infinite.

Leaving the shore is the first great challenge, but it is only necessary to begin to face the challenge. Even though the challenges may become greater later, we are assured that we shall be given everything we need to face them. We begin by saying the mantra. Saying the mantra is always to be beginning, to be returning to the first step. We learn in time that there is only one step between us and God.

Opening our hearts to the spirit of Christ is the only way into the certain knowledge that that step has been taken. Christ has taken it in himself. He himself is the step between God and man because he is God and man. The language we use to express this mystery, the greatest and fundamental mystery of the human race and all time, is pathetically inadequate — as the theological controversies down through the centuries have shown. No language or concept or metaphor can express the mystery of Christ, because Christ is the full embodiment of God, and there can be no adequate expression of God except his own self-expression. The only way to know Christ is to enter his personal mystery, leaving ideas and words behind. We leave them behind in order to enter the silence of full knowledge and love to which meditation is leading each of us.   —PC 110–17

One of the words used to describe the purpose of meditation is "enlightenment." We meditate to become "enlightened."

St. John in his gospel describes the purpose of the coming of Christ as being to banish the darkness. The power of his personal light is so great that the darkness cannot overcome it.

Yet we are all aware that there is still much darkness in our world. We hear every day of terrible injustice, of feuds, of blind greed and insane destructiveness. We see all this at both the personal and political level, between our neighbors at home or abroad. Not so many of us however are aware of the residual darkness within ourselves. We need to recognize that we too have a dark side. We have a self-negating capacity to live at a level that we know is unworthy of our human destiny as persons who are images of God. When we begin to meditate, we soon come to understand that we cannot enter into the experience of meditation with just part of our being. Everything that we are, the totality of our being, must be involved in this entry into wholeness itself, which realizes our own personal wholeness and harmony. Another way of expressing this is to say that every still-darkened part of our being must come into the light. We do not meditate just to develop our religious side or our moral capacity. Meditation is the way into harmonious integration of our total self with the whole of reality.

A truly spiritual man or woman is in harmony with every capacity they possess. That is why the spiritual person does everything with the greatest possible spirit of perfection. Which leads to the greatest possible love and so the greatest possible joy. The reason is this — meditation is not the process whereby we try to see the light. In this life we cannot see the light fully and continue to live. Our present concern should be for the light to see us, to search and know us; to be enlightened. Meditation is the process whereby we come into the light. As a natural consequence of this process we begin to see everything, the whole interlacing reality of life, by the power of the light.

At this point we need to check our language. What is this "light"? What does this great spiritual symbol mean? What is it that "enlightens" us and changes the way we perceive daily reality? Jesus tells us that the power of "light" is love. And so for the Christian meditator the test of our progress in meditation is simply how far we are moving into the enlightened state of seeing everyone and every interrelated thing by the light of God. Seeing by the light of his universal love makes us loving toward them all, too. Not judging, not rejecting, but seeing every person and, indeed, the whole of creation by this light, we must discover love's source in our own heart. We must know ourselves loved: this is the knowledge of Christian enlightenment. —HC 45–46

5

Embracing the World

John Main was firmly convinced of the social dimension of meditation. Experience had taught him of the self-contradictions, selfishness, and denial that must be faced if the world, so evidently heading for disaster, is to change its course. He believed it could change direction provided people recover their interiority and, with it, their sense of life as sacred mystery.

His teaching of meditation in all its sublime simplicity addresses the need of modern people to remember that mystery. Religion depends on faith and faith depends on personal experience. The institutional tragedy of Christianity today is its preoccupation with orthodoxy of belief and its neglect of that openness to mystery which is the essence of both faith and religion. Religion without spiritual experience atrophies, as the steady erosion of mainline Christian denominations and the proliferation of evangelical, nondenominational groups demonstrate.

John Main liked to quote St. Clement of Rome's cry to the early persecuted and marginalized Christians: "O Christian, recognize your dignity!" The Christian life for John Main sets us against the pessimism and death wish that lurk in the depths of the human psyche and are so often expressed socially in vio-

lence and injustice. The mission of Christianity, as he saw it, is not to convert people to the church but to resensitize the world to the presence of the spirit within the human person. It does this not by insisting on its own answers but by keeping people open to the important questions — the openness that is the essence of faith.

This mission of Christ is shared with his disciples through time and space; that mission is the church. John Main's contemplative vision of reality leads him to an understanding of the church that is strikingly positive for the modern Christian. His sense of the church is radical both in seeing the church's importance for the destiny of humanity and in its affirmation that the church is fully experienced through the individual in community rather than through the institution. Offering an alternative to the static, bureaucratic model of the church, he calls upon the organic metaphors of the New Testament. The church is a "living creature" engendered by the redemptive activity of Christ and kept alive both by the Holy Spirit (Christ's medium of self-transmission) and our response to the Spirit. Christians are "living stones" of a spiritual temple rather than just members of an institution. "Born again in Christ" they enjoy a kind of fellowship that is new to humanity and that itself creates the church. The church for John Main, then, did not mean just a global religion, certainly not a particular denomination, nor even the great cosmic mystery, but the local community in which the Christian is in relationship with others and lives out a deepening experience of conversion.

The church is an experience of spiritual community that gives each of us new power to know and to love. Far from smothering individuality, it allows true personhood and mature relationship to develop. Its fellowship expresses in human terms the nature of divine life.

When he looks at the troubles of modern Christianity, especially in its historical homelands, John Main does not see the future renewal in terms of organizational reform. As far as the Catholic Church was concerned, he felt that this had been achieved at the Second Vatican Council. What remains to be accomplished is a new collective experience of depth. This is where John Main's monastic identity and point of view are most evident. From his own inner experience and his knowledge of community he understood that the church is essentially a sign of the transformation of consciousness. Holiness in this perspective is not primarily a moral quality. It is not about conformity but openness to presence. The church is a school of prayer, a training ground for holiness. If it saw itself in this way, it would be less concerned with success, numbers, and its media image. It would know itself as the conscious presence of Christ in the world, a presence that can never be institutionalized.

LIVING TRADITION

East and West

The thousands of young Westerners who travel to the East go seeking a living experience of the mystery of God they could not find in the church in the West. Some, no doubt, do find genuine guides and teachers of prayer with whom they can, if they are serious themselves, learn to meditate. But many others do not have such fortune and are left confused and even more alienated than before. It is clear that these young people do not reject God. Why have they then rejected the Christian religious structure of the West?

Perhaps the reason is that we in the West have become too religious rather than truly spiritual. What so many today are seeking is a humble yet authoritative witness to the absolute. Our call as monks is always a call to the experience of God in Christ. This experience has to be personal if it is to be real.

Our contemporaries in the West will come to our monasteries only when they are convinced that this is the primary reason for our existence — that we do truly seek God as our very first responsibility.

In the depth of our being we are relentlessly summoned to realize our union with the Spirit of God in whom we have our being. It is a mysterious sign of our age that this intuition is accepted without question by so many of the thousands who seek the way outside conventional religion. They have leaped back in a moment to a basic spiritual truth that centuries of organized religion has obscured for so many. It must, then, seem as absurd to them as it did to St. Paul to find Christians "morbidly keen on mere verbal questions and quibbles" that make us lose grip of the Truth. Religion without spiritual experience becomes atrophied and futile, as St. James realized. But to place meditation at the center of our religious life is not to deny the value of religion. As St. Paul knew also, it affirms it: of course religion does yield high dividends, he tells us — but only to the individuals whose resources are within them.

What our encounter with India and the East is teaching us is something we should never have forgotten — that the essential Christian experience is beyond the capacity of any cultural or intellectual form to express. This is the "glorious liberty of the children of God": no restriction. It became so clear to us talking with Father Bede Griffiths that this experience has to be restored to the heart of the church if she is to face creatively the challenges before her: the challenge of the renewal of her contemplative religious life, the challenge of finding unity in the Spirit with all Christian communions, the challenge of embracing the non-Christian religions with the universal love of Christ present in the hearts of all people and which she has a special duty to release and identify. To meet these challenges each one of us must be personally rooted in the experience of God that Jesus personally knows and shares with us all through his Spirit.

We do not earn this experience or create it from our own resources; it is for us to prepare for the grace of its giving. Our fidelity to meditation is our preparation, our patient and ever deepening openness to the mystery that fills and contains us. We have to be still. We have to be silent. We have to stand reverently in the cave of our hearts, the palace of God's kingdom within us.   —LH 102–3

It is one of the great dangers of religious people that they can feel so at home in their verbal formulas and their rituals that they fail to recognize such an absolutely fundamental value of the spiritual life as silence. The most refreshing and encouraging aspect of the interfaith service held to greet the Dalai Lama in the cathedral in Montreal was precisely the recognition of this value by several thousand people of different traditions when we meditated together in deep silence for about twenty minutes. It was at the same time an absolute and an ordinary occasion, a realization of unity in spirit.   —PC 27–28

Living Tradition

What I am suggesting is this: our society has become personalistic after a long history of dominant legalism and intellectualism. But at the same time it has lost a vital contact with its tradition and so it is pursuing an experience-centered course, not bad in itself as I have said, but presently lacking the stability and centrality the tradition can give it. What the church must proclaim is that this tradition is the central human experience of the Mystery writ large. To be in contact with the tradition is not to forgo the validity of our own experience but to have the grace of the opportunity to make our experience complete — by making it other-centered, purifying it of all egoism, all self-preoccupation. The tradition — and this is the community of the faithful as the Person of Christ — is the universal hinge upon which we swing away from ourselves to God. At no time in history has the richness of this tradition been more universally available to us. Why, then, do we remain so trapped in the prison of our ego and why does our experience, deep as it is, fail to reach its full potential in the vision of God — no longer "seeing God" but being robed in the power of God's vision?

—LH 107–8

One of the basic insights was to see in a new way the great importance of meditation to the living tradition of the faith. All of us, at least in the West and especially those brought up in Christian homes, received the tradition as part of our general cultural heritage and as part of the whole system of values and ways of seeing life that we take more or less for granted. The basic Christian values have become so essential a part of our overall formation that it is easy to identify them with a particular type of society and so to lose sight of them as our society and culture evolve. When the Christian tradition loses contact with its own inner dynamic, it not only cannot lead people to build a new society on their experience of these basic values, but it even tends to lose its own self-confidence — the authority that derives from its living contact with its author. The faith tradition we receive on our entry into the Christian community depends for its authenticity and effectiveness on personal experience. It is a tradition of powerful richness and significance and one that is never stale because it is part of a pattern that is still in formation. Each generation, like each individual, has a different past. The perspective of history is in constant change. But all this resourcefulness and dynamism is only potential until it is realized or activated by the personal faith-decisions undertaken by each individual as a maturing member of the Christian family. And this decision or commitment of faith is not merely intellectual or dialectical. It is not that we decide to "believe" in the ideas of the Christian tradition. It is much rather that we have the courage and, in a real sense, the recklessness to open ourselves to the unknown, the unfathomable and truly mysterious dimension of the tradition. We allow ourselves, in the full biblical sense, to "know" the mystery or, even better, to be known by it. To allow ourselves to do this (a better way of putting it than to say make ourselves do it) is to follow the fundamental gospel precept of becoming simple, of becoming childlike, of becoming awake. It is no small cause for wonder that despite the fact that the tradition has been influential for so long those in its mainstream so easily forget that these are the fundamental tenets of the gospel of Jesus — that faith is not a matter of exertion but of openness.

We need to see faith in this way as openness, and to see it as a positive, creative, sensitive way of being — miles apart from mere passivity or quietism. The effectiveness of all doing depends on the quality of being we enjoy. And to be open implies certain other qualities: such as being still, because we cannot be open to what is here if we are always running after what we think is there; such as being silent, because we cannot listen or receive unless we give our whole attention; such as being simple, because what we are being open to is the wholeness, the integrity of God. This condition of openness as the blend of stillness, silence, and simplicity is the condition of prayer, our nature and being in wholesome harmony with the being and nature of God in Jesus.

Meditation is our way to this condition of being fully human, fully alive — a condition we all are called to. To meditate is to stand in the middle — *stare in Medio* — and to be conscious that the center is not ourselves but God. And in meditation, therefore, we enter into the living stream of faith that gives meaning to and realizes the tradition that has formed us and which we are responsible for transmitting to those not yet born. We do so by entering the state of faith where we are solely and exclusively open to the personal presence of the living Christ within, knowing that presence fully and personally, beyond the limitations of language and thought — knowing it "though it is beyond knowledge." This sort of knowledge is of a different order from the sort we acquire and store in studying history, in scientific research, in reading poetry. It is not our objective knowledge of God as an object and could never be because God can never be known as an object — a truth proclaimed by the Christian tradition since Irenaeus, who tells us, "Without God you cannot know God." Only God can know himself and we are called to participate in his knowledge of himself — a calling made feasible because of our union with Jesus. But we have to remind ourselves that this "knowledge" is not a mere intellectualist comprehension of God's greatness, his absoluteness, and his compassion. God's self-knowledge is his love, the love that is in the Trinity and that is the basic energy and prototype of all creation. God is love, St. John tells us, so we are called by love into love.   —LH 63–65

The Monastic Way

For St. Benedict, the first quality we all require if we would respond to Christ and open to his life in our hearts is the capacity to listen. The first word of the Rule is "Listen!" And as you all know, this capacity is one of the great fruits of meditation, which teaches us that the condition of true listening is silence. We can listen to the word spoken to us by another only if we ourselves are silent of all words. The wonder of Benedict's spirit as it speaks to us in the Rule is that his understanding of the prayerful heart is so naturally and humanly integrated into his whole vision of life. He does not see silence in the monastery, for example, just as a regulation to be obeyed, but wisely knows that there are times when charity will demand words. Instead, he sees silence as the fundamental condition of our heart, attentiveness to a reality larger than the limits of our immediate

activities or concerns, a heart wrapped in silence and wholly attentive to the word of the Master. We are not attentive to this
merely at set times: our attentiveness is the way we live, our silence is the state of being in which we respond to the gift of life.
It is one of the great creative paradoxes of the Spirit that it is
only in this attentive listening, this silent openness, that we can
at all respond to the mystery of our experience with the appropriate response. Our busyness, our noisiness, our attempts to
provide for all contingencies are all the ways we try to reduce
the mystery of life to the status of a solvable problem — and in
these ways we so often miss the creative moment, fail to see the
gift as it opens before us. We lack the readiness on which the
necessary spontaneity of spirit depends. We become dreamers
of possibilities rather than tasters of real life.

Everyone is seeking a way. The problem is we so often
demand to accept the way only on our own terms. We see
ourselves as choosing God. We invite ourselves to the Master's banquet. And in so doing we are making an essentially
immature response to the gift of our own being, a childish assessment of the infinite potential of the Life that has called us
into being to share its own plenitude of joy. This is where our
tradition is of such importance, why we have to know ourselves
formed by and rooted in this progressive experience, why it has
to be personally known and retransmitted with the genuineness
of new discovery for every generation. The way of our tradition
is a heart opened to the infinite mystery of God by awakening
to itself. We awake in silence.   —LH 113–15

Visitors to the monastery often come with unclear motives.
They may not know where or how to begin a journey whose
call they can nevertheless neither evade nor shake off. So what
they first experience often surprises them. They think they
will find God in the terms they have imagined until then. But
instead they first find themselves — recognized, known, and

inexplicably loved. And because of that experience their expectations begin to change. They no longer seek a God of their own imagining. Instead, they begin to expand in the presence of the God they know to be beyond thought or image. They begin to realize that their seeking often served merely to lock them blindly into themselves and to tie them to the limitations of images. Far more wonderful, they now realize that God is seeking them. They must simply be still and allow themselves to be found. All this is, of course, something only experience can teach, and a loving community can provide the context for the discovery. The monk is one who follows through on this discovery in such a context. He is one who, by his own commitment to the journey, is called to help create and strengthen the community where others, maybe by a brief contact with it, can find their way.   —LH 72–73

To pray is to be open to the otherness of God. To love is to turn beyond self toward another. What summons us to this turning, this conversion of self-transcendence, is the Word of God. The text of Scripture before us leads us into the otherness of God and the monk faithful to his reading of Scripture has more capacity to witness to the reality of that otherness found in the living person of Jesus — the person who lives in our hearts, the inner person of each of us. Lectio [the meditative reading of Scripture practiced by monks], like every other aspect of the monastic life, is there to prepare us for the encounter with this person, for contact with his otherness. And more than contact, for it prepares us for the movement of transcendence right beyond ourselves and into the life of the Trinity, the communion of God, the mutual love that is God. Lectio prepares us for the mystery of God — a mystery that "eye has not seen, nor ear heard." We have to be clear that it does prepare us. The movement itself is accomplished by the redemptive love of Jesus that we encounter as our spirit opens fully to his life released in our hearts.

Our prayer is our openness of heart. We prepare to open our hearts by the fundamental quality of simplicity that we bring to our Lectio. The simplicity of the monk, as I have said, is his way to oneness with Jesus. And so Lectio is the great preparation for prayer that each monk builds into his life. It is also built into the corporate community life in the form of community Lectio and this is what we know as the Divine Office. The Office is, for the monks in assembly, their attentive, daily reading of the sacred texts of Scripture and the traditional interpretation of those texts by the church through the ages. It is always a sacred moment in the monastic day when the monks as one person, one in Christ, listen to the Word addressed to them. It is a moment that St. Benedict called monks to return to seven times a day.

It is, I think, essential that we understand the Divine Office as this preparation for prayer if we are to recover our monastic balance in the three elements of our life. Upon this balance depends our making-present the full richness of our tradition and so also our relevance to the world. This is in no way to play down the sacredness of the Divine Office. Quite the reverse, what it reveals is the true meaning and effective value of the Office as the great community context for preparing the heart of each monk to be open to the same reality. It prepares them for the prayer that is the unity they share. It prepares them for the encounter with the otherness of God in silence and stillness — in what St. Benedict calls in the Rule, *oratio pura* — pure prayer. That is the prayer that is beyond thought, beyond imagination, beyond words — the prayer in which we are simply in the presence.   — CL 132–33

Unless someone has had the experience of being loved they are wounded. They are unalive at that center of their being where the awareness of God awakes to realize them as persons and to release their divine gift of loving others, of turning away from self. The monastery shares deeply in the responsibility of healing those who — more and more in our society — have been wounded by the nonexperience of love. But also the monastery is a place where in all simplicity and steadiness a living witness is being made to the human capacity for love, and the possibility of being transformed by the direct experience of the love of God — at the center, in the heart of every person. It is a place then that testifies to the liberty of God to act as he will, to transcend the laws and conventions by which people have to limit the ordinary working of their lives and relationships. A monastery is a center of prayer only to the degree that it is a community of love. The prayer is an openness to the love; the monastery is the communication of that love to all within it and to all who encounter it. It is above all a fully human society that goes beyond materialistic conventions only to be the more personal, the more human, and therefore to receive and share the inestimable gift of knowing the experience of being loved and so recognizing the power of love to heal and redeem. From this human experience a depth is opened up in people that is itself the depth of prayer. Confident in our own being because of the love of the brethren, we can then leave ourselves behind and enter into that depth which opens onto the limitlessness of love as the basic energy of all being.   — CL 96–97

I think that it is a grave mistake to read too many books on prayer or on the spiritual life. Not just because so many of them seem to contain such extraordinary statements, but because time is so precious. It is much better to spend our time in meditation than reading someone who is writing about someone else's writing of what it is like to pray. For St. Benedict, the call is not to be a great expert on all the latest paperbacks on spirituality. The call is to simple fidelity. "Let nothing be put before the work of God." Even the theory of the work of God.

Why should Benedict have his priorities so clear? I think that the reason is that he understands human nature so well. In the gospel Jesus tells us that if we want to find our true selves, that is, to make deep, real contact with the ground of our being, then the thing to do is to take up our cross and follow him. St. Benedict's Rule is a mirror of the Gospel, and he knows perfectly well that if we do attempt to go for self-fulfillment, self-advancement, self-perfection, the only result can be ruin.

As you read the Rule of St. Benedict I think you will see more and more that the vision he proposes is a difficult one for people of our age and generation. The reason is that his doctrine flies in the face of conventional wisdom. Does the person who comes to be a monk really seek God? The conventional wisdom urges us to go for self-fulfillment, self-understanding, and self-analysis. Even among Christians the cross is not spoken of in any very clear terms today. Yet if we do not tread that way and treat it faithfully there is nothing ahead but ruin. What we have to understand, those of us who try to follow the vision proclaimed by St. Benedict, by our way of meditation, is that our meditation is not there for our own self-perfection. We are not seeking to become spiritual experts. We are not seeking to become spiritual teachers. We are only seeking to be available to God, to be available to him in our prayer, in our reflection on the Word of God in Scripture, in our work and to have all this bound together by Divine Love.   —CL 59–60

THE CHURCH

I want to say something about the church. It is very important that we should find out exactly where we are in our relationship with the church. First of all if you ask yourself the question, "What is the church?" you are almost bound to come up with an idea that the church is something outside us, an entity or institution that is external to us. I think that when we begin to think about the church we have to ask ourselves not so much, "What is the church?" as "Who am I?" or, better still, "Who are we?" I think if we ask ourselves this question, the answer we arrive at concerning the church will not be a sterile, juridical one, speaking in terms of official membership, institution, hierarchy, and so forth. But we will begin to see that the church is itself a living creature that has come into being through the redemptive activity of Christ. And it is kept alive by a double pulse. First there is the pulse of the love of God that he extends continually to us — what St. Paul called the Spirit pleading for us. The second pulse is the pulse of our willing and whole-hearted acceptance of that love. In other words, allowing our hearts to beat in unison with his. And because our hearts beat in unison with his, they beat in unity, one with another. This is the way in which we allow his love to enter us, and what inspires us to bring that love to the world. So I think what we have got to see is, in the language of Scripture, that we are the living stones that make up the church. We ourselves are new creatures born in this newness of life because we have entered into this new fellowship, this new relationship with God and with one another.

A lot of people have reservations about this theology, because they see it as being excessively optimistic. They think it is a danger that we could become intoxicated by the optimistic freedom of thoughts like this. But I do not think any of us need to be reminded that if we have been born again in Christ, we do have this new relationship to one another, and this relationship creates the church. None of us, I think, needs to be reminded either that there is a certain dead, pessimistic weight in us that rebels against this daily transformation: the transformation that requires a continuous conversion to the person of Christ. And that ongoing turning is what makes a person more deeply Christian. What makes a person more effectively and more fully a member of the church is this constant deepening of one's conversion. That is a very different thing from just amassing increasing information about Christ or his church or just being obedient.

I suggest to you that the reason we have to ask the question "Who am I?" Or "Who are we?" is because if we do not open our deep selves to Christ and allow our whole lives to be transformed in Christ, we have at best only a very limited opportunity to find out who we really are. It seems to me that the church is above all a community in which a person has a new power to know and a new power to love. The invitation to join the church is an invitation to deeper, less isolated individuality, to deeper, more altruistic personal growth, and to deeper fulfillment. Each of us has a deeper power to know through faith, and a deeper power to love through charity. By entering the church's community of faith and love we know that we are known and that we are loved.

If we speak of the church in terms of a particular Christian church, such as the Roman Catholic Church, we must also have a complementary understanding of our own local church. Every spiritual community is in itself in some sense a microcosm of the church. I think we must all be very clear that the invitation to be a member of a faith community is an invitation to achieve one's own deepest, personal fulfillment, to become more perfectly the person one is called to be. We recognize that we will come to be the person we are called to be by being rooted in Christ, the one who is himself most deeply personal, and who reveals to us the fullness of the personhood of God. What we have to witness to is that in the church, in our communities, the individual can never live merely as an individual. We are bound to express what we are: one bound in love to others, in a love that is outward-looking and redeemed. The church, then, is not so much something outside us that we enter; it is rather the church that enters us, or emerges from deep within us. At baptism the bond of love unites us to Christ and to our fellow Christians. Christ enters us. It is only in this sense that we are born "into" the church.

I want to reflect for a moment upon some of the biblical images of the church to see if we can deepen our understanding of it by using the imagination of the Jewish people. One of the favorite descriptions of the church is that it is a temple constructed of living stones. That is a marvelous image of the church — that each of us has an integral function in it. Each of us is absolutely essential, whether as a little slate up on the roof keeping off the rain or as a great big foundation stone down below not seen above the surface but keeping the whole thing up. Or we may be like those people that all communities have, a kind of flying buttress on the outside. Whatever our function, we have an integral, essential role in the whole structure, and the whole structure is giving glory to God. So the idea of the temple is a magnificent and compelling image; but it does have the great disadvantage of being a static concept. And whether you are a flying buttress or a great foundation stone down below, you are just there — plonk! — and that is it. But our experience of being the church is something far more dynamic.

Another concept of the church which St. Paul likes is as the living body with Christ as its head. For St. John it is a living vine with the branches rooted in the true vine. It is a city with its origin in heaven. In these living examples of the vine and the body, I think we have the best image of the church. It is something that is constantly growing, developing, changing, but always drawing strength and direction from the true vine, from the head of the body, the Lord Jesus. Its root is deep in the ground of being.

An image of the church that I like very much myself is that of a bride constantly preparing to meet her spouse who is God. I was at home for the weddings of my three sisters, and each time the whole house was thrown into complete chaos because of the well-known vanity of my family. My sisters were always dashing back to take a last look in the mirror to see that their veil was exactly at the right angle or whatever it was, preparing to stagger everyone in the church with their astonishing beauty. The image of the bride constantly preparing to meet her spouse has a really dynamic element in it. We are always open to the love of Jesus, always open and prepared to be, as it were, his loved one.

What I want to stress by these examples is that all of us must accept the responsibility to be constantly creating and re-creating the church. That is an aspect of ecclesiology that we have not been so clear on in the past. The church is co-created by us. We have this responsibility. I can tell you a family story that illustrates how strongly some people love the church and how they feel "responsible" for it.

I have very rarely in my life heard a sermon interrupted by a parishioner — except by my father, who was a very wild Kerry-man. For a while we lived in London, and my father had a most beloved parish priest there who also came from Kerry. Everyone revered this man as a saint. But this priest was not very good at keeping financial accounts. In fact, he had a small parlor in the presbytery which he kept locked, and when the Sunday collections were taken in he just opened the door, threw what was in the plates into the room, and then locked the door again. When the milkman needed to be paid, or whatever it was, the priest would go in on his hands and knees and scoop out the money that was required. When the priest died having kept the accounts like this for twenty years or so, there was absolute chaos, so that the archbishop sent the most efficient priest in the diocese to try to sort the whole thing out. He was very nice, a somewhat correct and formal Englishman. My father was very, very disappointed when this poor fellow arrived after the death of the previous one. After he had been there a year, the Englishman got up to render an account of his stewardship, and he announced that when he had arrived in the parish things were in a state of terrible chaos caused by the previous priest, who had clearly been no financial manager. My father was getting rather upset. Then the new priest went on with his sermon from the pulpit denouncing his predecessor over and over again. To my mother's horror and to the utter horror of the entire congregation, the next thing you know my father jumped up saying, "Will you get down from there!" Now my father was a fairly formidable fellow. He was about six foot three with a big mop of curly black hair. The priest was unwise enough to try to argue with my father, at which time my father began striding up the church saying, "If you don't get down, I shall put you down!" The priest at that stage thought better of it, and he moved nippily to the altar, closing the altar rail door as he got inside. My father, I think, had some idea that he also was responsible for the church and for the good name of the man he loved who had been the pastor. In his own rather eccentric way he decided that he would accept that responsibility.

All of us have to come to a much more living view of the church in that or a similar real way: that we accept our responsibility. We cannot just sit back criticizing the bishops or the pope. We have our own responsibility to the church, and in that sense we create it. There must be constant interaction between all members of the Body of Christ that create it, and that is what makes, or should make, the church such an extraordinarily rich, vital, enriching, and vitalizing society to belong to.

We must recover the sense of the power of Christ at work in the church. For example, if you look at the letter to the Ephesians, you find very clearly in the theology of Paul that Christ has entered into our own death. Christ has liberated us from death by being exalted at the right hand of the Father. What St. Paul shows us is that Christ here and now calls forth this liberating power in and through the church — not the church as some hierarchic, static institution, but the church that is the

family of God, the household of God, the redeemed of God —
the church as those who know that they are the redeemed of
God and who know that they are part of his household. Listen
to his words: "You are no longer aliens or foreign visitors. You
are citizens like all the saints and part of God's household. You
are part of the building that has the apostles and the prophets
for its foundation. And Jesus Christ is himself the main corner-
stone. And as every structure is aligned upon him all grow into
one holy temple in the Lord." Then he adds, using the present
tense of the verb, "and you too, in him, are being built into a
house where God lives in the Spirit."

What is abundantly clear for St. Paul is that the church is the
continuation among humankind of what God effected in Christ.
And this continuation of the Christ-life is achieved through the
activity of the Spirit. The Spirit is, as it were, not sent merely
into an institution; the Spirit is sent into the hearts of men and
women not as mere individuals, but as a community. Listen
again to Ephesians: "For he [God] brought us back to life in
Christ and he raises us up with him and he gives us a place with
him in heaven in Christ Jesus." In other words, for St. Paul the
church is constituted by those who recognize the living Christ
in their midst, the living Spirit of Christ in their hearts.

All the images of the Bible have this in common, that the
Christian has his or her meaning as a Christian because of
belonging to this new community, this new family, this new fellowship. It is the fellowship of those who recognize the Lord
Jesus and his Spirit in their hearts and in the hearts of their
fellow members of the church, the community. The church is
not a community which destroys or smothers individuality. The
church is a community in which we find our true individuality
through community. It is especially in St. John that we see this
meaning of the church as the fellowship, though "fellowship"
is a very poor word in modern English. We do not have a good
one-word translation of the Greek *koinonia* in modern English.

For St. John the church is this friendly, warm-hearted, loyal, mutually caring fellowship which has come down from heaven in order to create among humankind a society that is an expression of the fellowship of the union that exists among the three persons of the most Holy Trinity itself. The Johannine version is that the most perfect community is the most Holy Trinity, and that the church is composed of those who enter into this relationship in union with the most Holy Trinity. The church in this sense is the Word become flesh in order to serve the Father and in order to enter into the total service of humankind.

For St. John the church, as the Christ-presence in the world, is above all to be recognized by its dedication to the teaching of Jesus and by its service of others. For John, it is through the service of Jesus that this new fellowship is brought into being. It is a fellowship in his victimhood, in his service of us, and above all a fellowship with his risen life. This centering of our lives on Christ in the Spirit of the Father is the central theme of John's priestly prayer of Christ: "May they all be one, so that the world may believe that it was you who sent me." Here is a point that we have got to take very much to heart. Our unity in the church, and in our communities, is the touchstone of our effectiveness in proclaiming the gospel. For John it is our unity that is the great sign of the church as the presence in this world of the Father, of Jesus, and of the Holy Spirit.

Mistakes in the church down through history have smothered individuality and made the church into an authoritarian institution; most of those mistakes have been made because Christians have not seen the importance of this unity. But it is a unity that can never be brought about by force. It is a unity that cannot be brought about by merely organizational structures. It is not uniformity; it is a unity that has to be based above all in the reality of the Spirit which is apprehended in the hearts of the individual members of the church. And so the central idea in the Johannine theology is of union with Christ and of the union of Christ within the unity of the most Holy Trinity. For the early church, Christian worship was simply the way for men and women to enter most deeply into this union.

I would like to end for now by stressing that it is in the church, with that Spirit-dimension to it, that we find the possibility for the greatest fullness in our own lives. We have to be aware of that fullness and ensure that it is known as a real and present possibility.   —AW 37–44

The Christian Mission

If our Christianity is more than just another ideology on a comparative religion program, if it is a life we receive and mediate, we have to ask ourselves a question: Why is it that the power of this risen life of Jesus is not being mediated through us to transform the negative energies of modern people's self-rejection into the positive awareness of the depth and richness of their own spirit?

In the ancient myth of the Fisher King, the land has been blighted by a curse that has frozen all the waters and turned the earth to stone. No power in the land can lift the curse, and the king sits silently fishing through a hole in the ice, despondently waiting. One day a stranger approaches and asks the king the redemptive question. Immediately the waters thaw and the earth softens.

Religious people have so often pretended to have all the answers. They have seen their mission as being to persuade, to enforce, to level differences, and perhaps even to impose uniformity. There is really something of the Grand Inquisitor in most religious people. But when religion begins to bully or to insinuate, it has become unspiritual because the first gift of the Spirit, creatively moving in human nature, is freedom and frankness; in biblical language, liberty and truth. The mission of modern

Christians is to resensitize our contemporaries to the presence of a spirit within themselves. We are not teachers in the sense that we are providing answers that we have looked up in the back of a book. We are truly teachers when, having found our own spirit, we can inspire others to accept the responsibility of their own being, to undergo the challenge of their own innate longing for the Absolute, to find their own spirit. — WS 25–26

A group of Christians who meet together to meditate, to pray, to worship is not just a mere social gathering. It is a group aware of its power: a power that arises from the transcendent reality of the presence of the Lord Jesus in their midst. The purpose of their meeting is, before anything else, to attend to the reality of this presence, to deepen their silent receptivity to it, to make it (what it already is) the supreme reality of their lives. So the members of the group are other-centered, turned away from themselves toward the living Lord. And the group then becomes truly a community — like that described to us at the end of the second chapter of Acts: "A sense of awe was everywhere...all whose faith had drawn them together held everything in common...with unaffected joy."

The Christian group, then, must always be aware of its ultimate meaning being beyond itself. The social, cultural, or ceremonial form of the group must never become something to be preserved or, above all, something to be possessed: all truly Christian response requires detachment that helps us to enjoy externals while never ceasing to concentrate on the essential reality. And, of course, the reality is the transcending reality — the power of the risen Lord Jesus. All this is, of course, so obvious, but it was just this proclamation of the essential liberty of the spirit of Jesus that seemed such a threat to the Pharisees. And our tendency, too, is often to opt for the static security of an established order, what we know and what we feel safe with. The tragedy of such an option is that it does not even allow us to remain static: we go into decline because we have opted to evade the only real security there is — the rock of Christ, the dynamos of God, the glorious liberty of the children of God. Our glory and liberty as Christians is just that we have been enabled to make this positive option, to turn away from ourselves and our anxiety, and what has enabled us to do so is that we have been turned around by Jesus.   —LH 45–46

Today the rediscovery we need is not primarily a religious one. We don't need, in the first place, to recover our identity in any superficial religious sense with any superficial religious demarcations — for example as good Baptists, Anglicans, Catholics, or even Atheists. What we need is an experience of depth, to fill the surface with identity, with meaning, with purpose and shape once again. This experience ensues when we make contact with our own inner spiritual nature, when we enter the structure of reality as it is established in our deepest center, where the Spirit of God, God in all his fullness, dwells in love. Out of that contact — and the word is "contact" much more than "contemplation" — arises a deeply rooted and sane spiritual sense that will naturally communicate itself in the whole gamut of our religious, social, interpersonal, and personal living responses to reality.   —LH 47

We can describe the journey as one from self-consciousness (the primary distraction and narrowness of the ego) to self-awareness (the clarified and expansive knowledge of our participation in reality). The church itself is called to be a special sign of this transformation of consciousness. It is called beyond concern for its own image, its own success, or its own influence. The church is itself only when it is aware that it is the conscious presence of Christ in this world. This consciousness is the basis of its transcendent nature that can never be wholly institutionalized. The church has always been vitalized by men and women who have the courage to tread this austere way, the way beyond self into the consciousness of Christ. The tradition that preserves, nurtures, and communicates this awareness of God in Christ is the tradition of the Spirit present in the church, enlivening the church. All this suggests to us the primacy of the Spirit over the letter. Letters can build up into the living Word that the church must utter in every generation only if the energy of new life is set free to enliven the letter, and this new life must be free in the depths of our hearts. As Christians, we must speak a living word to our contemporaries. It must be a word that is authoritative, not authoritarian, a word that is not sectarian, but is truly catholic. We can speak this word only when we are alive with the life of Christ. The church as envisioned in the New Testament is primarily a community of vitalized and enlightened brethren, illumined and charged with a life beyond their own — a life arising from the power of the risen Christ. The writers of the New Testament everywhere call on the early Christians to be open to this power. We in our turn, carrying on a tradition greater than ourselves, must call on our contemporaries to enter the dynamism of the marriage between God and humanity in Christ. But we can do so only when we ourselves have undertaken the pilgrimage to this union by our own selfless commitment to the pilgrimage.

What each of us must learn in the experience of our meditation is that the power of the pilgrimage is in fact inexhaustibly present. It takes only one step of faith for us to know that from our own experience. The important thing to remember is that one faltering but actual step is more valuable than any number of journeys performed in the imagination. As beginners we have to accept a certain distance between what we say externally and what we seek internally. As we begin to tread the path that unites surface and depth, we have to recognize that we are limited. That we are sinners. What all this means is that we must understand that although we are setting out, we are only

setting out. We have not yet arrived. Nothing is more likely to
make us arrogant than to imagine that we have arrived before
we have actually left. Leave we must. When we reflect on the
necessity of this commitment it illumines the real opportunity
and responsibility we have. Christ is consciously present in time
only to the degree that we, his brothers and sisters, open our
minds and hearts to him in this world, only to the degree that
we have undertaken the commitment to be real, to be still, to
persist in reality. When we do embrace this commitment, the
church becomes in the first place not an institution, not an or-
ganization, not a hierarchy, but the Body of Christ, filled in its
every limb with this vital and vitalizing power. Not only filled
with his power but — in the way of all conscious life — alive to
that life in full self-awareness.   —PC 77–78

I recently took part in a huge Catholic conference at the
Anaheim Conference Center in southern California. It was
an extraordinary experience in many ways. There were about
eighteen thousand people participating, all, it seemed to me, seriously interested in deepening the Christian dimension of their
lives.

They were responding, I suppose, in a typically Catholic way.
Each evening I would get little notes under my door saying "the
Sacred Heart invites you to drinks in room 1222," or "the Little
Flower will have a happy hour tomorrow evening." Yet I was
deeply moved by the last group I spoke to which consisted of
about eight thousand people. We all meditated together, and
their openness to become so silent was really inspiring.

My time there made me feel that the great problem we face
today is one of commitment. For the Christian this often seems
to be a question of committing oneself to certain beliefs or the
behavior based on those beliefs. Much of our religious response
is indeed based primarily upon our beliefs. But I have come to
feel that what we "believe" is not really that important. Belief is

like the tip of the iceberg. What matters is faith. For the Christian this means our deep commitment to Christ to the point of self-transcendence, at the very bedrock of our being.

Beliefs have to be couched in language. And language is necessary to keep the world going, of course — especially large conferences. I doubt whether eighteen thousand people would come a long way just to be silent together!

When I was studying eucharistic theology the key word was "transubstantiation." Since then all sorts of words, including "transfinalization," have been proposed by theologians as more suitable for portraying what it means. Words define beliefs. Words change. And so beliefs change. Beliefs are certainly secondary to faith, which does not change. This is our faith — meaning our transcendental commitment — to Jesus Christ. The task of life is to make contact with this faith, to reach what is essential by going beyond everything that is peripheral. The clear message of the New Testament is that Jesus Christ is essential and that what he communicates to us is his essence — his own being.

However, language like this — being, essence, and so on — can quickly lead to confusion. Meditation is of such supreme importance because it does not rest content with the mere formulations and propositions of language. It goes beyond the sign-realm of language and to the reality, the rock-bed of meaning who is Christ. "So come to him, our living stone — the stone rejected by people but choice and precious in the sight of God. Come, and let yourselves be built, as living stones, into a spiritual temple; become a holy priesthood, to offer spiritual sacrifices to God through Jesus Christ."

These words of St. Peter characterize the perennial call to faith for the Christian. We have ourselves to understand, and we have to communicate to our contemporaries, that this journey of faith is a journey of value. We discover that each of us, your reading this and I writing it, is precious in the sight of

God. This journey is possible for us even as ordinary persons of average talents and abilities.

We are called to tread this inner pilgrimage. Rooting our life in the spiritual reality is part of the plan of salvation — the meaning of the universe — revealed and actually completed in Jesus. Our task is simply to get on to the wavelength of this achievement. We do not have to accomplish it ourselves — to try to would be the highest hubris.

Putting ourselves into harmony with him is the work of the mantra. The mantra is a tuning device, a harmonic to help us to resonate with Jesus. By its means we are enabled, as St. Peter puts it, to let ourselves be built as living stones into a spiritual temple. By our commitment to meditating daily we take this option. By setting aside these two half-hours we move from the realm of materialistic expectations and conditions in order to enter the supreme reality of God revealed in Jesus. Reality does not exist outside of us, or even inside us. It is the heart where all dualities are resolved, and there is simply God, perfect wholeness.

During the conference in California I was most struck by the desperate need the world has for people who are rooted and grounded in faith. This means, for us, to be rooted in Christ as people who know the spiritual reality that is beyond knowledge and yet to which we are summoned as our personal destiny. People who realize the grandeur of that reality and calling are utterly humble and yet confident of the goodness and compassion of God. People who are confident without humility can be dangerous. Such religious confidence can be the most dangerous of all. But the world desperately needs people whose confidence is rooted in the humility of love. Such people, who undertake the pilgrimage into the true security of love, become grace for the world — for their friends and family, which is our first world. They are grace for the world at large as well, because this pilgrimage is a journey into sanity. Health and wholeness bestow the real, not the mock or artificial, value which has so deluded us today.

The ultimate value is God's love for each of us as well as for all creation. These two are really one, as God, being one, does not divide his love. He loves all or nothing, and does so equally because he loves absolutely. Human value — and God's love for us gives us this value — is personal. Faith, which is the transcendent point of encountering this love, must also be utterly personal. It must be your own faith, not somebody else's belief you have inherited or absorbed. You will encounter this faith in your own heart and in doing so meet God in the heart of Jesus.

The congress reminded me again of the importance for Christians of regaining a real sense of the magnificence of our calling.

"You are a chosen race, a royal priesthood, a dedicated nation, and a people claimed by God for his own, to proclaim the triumphs of him who called you out of darkness into his marvelous light. You are now the people of God, who once were not his people; outside his mercy once, you have now received his mercy."

Every time we meditate, alone or in a group, we respond to this call from darkness into his marvelous light.

—WMF 48–50

Somebody asked me at one of the meetings how meditation fitted in with the vision of the whole human race in its movement back to God through evolution and through free will. Is the Christian one of the elect, the tiny minority from among all races and generations who will awaken to God? And if so, does that mean that the Christian meditator is one of the inner track among the elect? It is an important question.

Every day I am more amazed at the range and variety of people who really hear the message of the teaching about meditation, who hear it from some deep and perhaps unsuspected stillness within themselves. And I am even more inspired that so many remain faithful to the discipline and the fidelity that makes the hearing really significant. They are people of all ages and backgrounds, educational, social, and religious. But they have discovered a common center, Christ, who lives in their hearts and in the heart of creation.

It would not be easy to generalize about what else they have in common. It is certainly nothing as superficial as an I.Q. rating or an interest in things religious. The wonder of the community of those on the pilgrimage is that it is really only their experience of faith that makes them seem the same. And the very wonder is that this faith is pure, unpredictable, invincible, and pure gift. That much we know, but according to what purpose or design the gift is given we are much less knowledgeable. The phenomenon of God's self-revelation and embodiment among mankind is the purest of mysteries, knowable but beyond understanding. To know it is to be made real and to be set at peace. To strive to understand it is to strive vainly to go beyond the limits of what is the specifically human reality.

Nevertheless, although this may seem to be pointing toward a spiritual elitism, it actually reinforces the solidarity, the interdependence, and the equality of the whole human family. Precisely because our capacity to hear and to respond, the capacity we call faith, is pure inexplicable gift, it is no cause for pride. Because the source of the gift is God, it cannot be purely arbitrary or without meaning.

The meaning is this: by hearing and responding, by pursuing the call of poverty of spirit and purity of heart, we discover that within the depths of our being we fulfill our part of the divine plan for the whole of humankind. The mantra is, as experience proves, an act of pure love, universal love. All those who meditate faithfully through all the personal storms and challenges of their personal life begin to know this. They come also to know that they are meditating through the crises and tragedies of their world. Indeed the further they go on their way, the closer they realize they are to the whole which is more than the sum of the parts. It is so because the Spirit moves among it, giving it that completion, that redemption which is the center of God's design. The communion we discover in the solitude of our own hearing and responding is not only communion with ourselves. That is perhaps the first we have of it — a deeper personal harmony and freedom. But it persists beyond, to the communion we share with all men and women, with all the dead and all the living and the yet unborn. With them we share the great and mysterious gift of life in the flesh and in the Spirit. And as we awaken to this deeper and higher sense of wholeness we sense the ultimate all-embracing communion which contains all this and of which these are epiphanies. The communion we have with God and the communion within God — this is the great truth we encounter. All we can say in the end is what we said at the beginning — that the meaning of life is the mystery of love.

Because of the incorporation of the whole — an incorporation that has both material and spiritual dimensions — every experience in the human family influences the whole. This is why St. Paul calls the early Christians "to weep with those who weep and to rejoice with those who rejoice." Violence, injustice, and all suffering anywhere within the Body of Christ affect and implicate us all. The reality is that we are not isolated. We are one with the One. We are one with all.   —PC 99–101

6

One Hundred Sayings
on Prayer, God, and Love

John Main was a modern desert father. The style of teaching of the desert fathers of the third and fourth centuries was essentially experiential. The great abbas and ammas used stories and brief statements to convey what they knew words could easily distort. They taught more by example than by words. John Main used to recommend that people read as little as possible about meditation, especially in the early stages of practice. The famous "Sayings of the Desert Fathers" were pithy summaries of their teaching. Their disciples would memorize and chew them mentally and in their heart. So it is appropriate to close this anthology with a selection of "sayings" by John Main, a spiritual guide for those in the modern desert, drawn from both his oral and written teaching.

In meditation we are all beginners.   —WS 49

We need the wisdom to search into the depth of things.
                                                       —IC 313

The mystery into which meditation leads us is a personal mystery, the mystery of our own personhood which finds its completion in the person of Christ.   —WS xii

Meditation is the very simple process by which we prepare ourselves in the first instance to be at peace with ourselves so that we are capable of appreciating the peace of the Godhead within us.   —WS 1

The task of meditation is to bring all of this mobile and distracted mind to stillness, silence, and concentration, to bring it, that is, into its proper service.   —WS 9

By means of the mantra we leave behind all passing images and learn to rest in the infinity of God himself.   —WS 16

Saying the mantra is the process of polishing the mirror within us so that our hearts become fully open to the work of God's love for us, fully reflecting the light of that love.   —WS 20

Saying the mantra is like dropping anchor.   —WMF 43

Meditation is our way of leaving behind all the illusions about ourselves, about others, and about God which we have either created for ourselves or received from the past.   —WS 23

Meditation is the prayer of faith because we have to leave ourselves behind before the Other appears and without the prepackaged guarantee that He will appear.   —WS 23

In meditation we must have the courage to attend solely to the Absolute, the abiding, and the central. To transcend we must be still. The stillness is our pilgrimage and the way of the pilgrim is the mantra.   —WS 29

The stillness of mind and body to which the mantra guides us is a preparation for entering this silence and for our progression through the spheres of silence — to see with wonder the light of our own spirit, and to know that light as something beyond our spirit and yet the source of it.   — WS 31

In saying the mantra we lay down our life for the sake of Him we have not yet seen.   — WS 31

Our death consists in the relentless simplicity of the mantra and the absolute renunciation of thought and language at the time of our meditation.   — WS 40

The mantra stills the mind and summons all our faculties to the resolution of a single point. At that point we know the "condition of complete simplicity that demands not less than everything."   — WS 44

The multiplicities of thought and the mobility of words all find their resolution in the one little word, the mantra.   — WS 47

In meditation we turn the searchlight of consciousness off ourselves.   — WS 51

The mantra is an ancient tradition, the purpose of which is to accept the invitation that Jesus makes to us.   — WS 52

Each time we meditate we return to the grounding conscious- ness of being.   — IC 237

The poverty and joy of our word leads us into the sea of the reality of God, and once there it keeps us simply in the current of the Spirit and leads us to a place unknown to us where we know ourselves in him, in his eternal now.   — IC 340

Meditation is a way of growth because what we are growing into is life itself.   —IC 325

We have to forget, to unknow everything we have been if we are to bring ourselves to completeness.   —IC 328

We can become fully present to the now of the divine moment only if we can leave the past behind totally.   —IC 328

Purity of heart is simplicity realized.   —FA

Meditation is a continuous breakthrough into the present moment of God.   —IC 329

The significance and quality of what we do depends upon our capacity for simply being.   —IC 320

Conversion is to the spiritual life what revolution is to the political life. . . . The ideal revolution is peaceful. It occurs in a society that recognizes the necessity for change.   —IC 305

Meditation is so important because we can come to the truth only if we have the courage to face it.   —IC 309

Every new strategy of the ego has to be laughed at and dismissed.   —WU 43

Meditation is a return to our original innocence.   —MC

As breathing is for the body, meditation is for the spirit.
                    —IC 309

The door to silence is the mantra.   —PC

The experience of poverty is only the beginning.   —BW

Silence is not just a matter of keeping our tongues still but much more of achieving a state of alert stillness in our mind and heart.   —WS 8

It requires nerve to become really quiet.   —WS 23

As we enter the silence within us we are entering a void in which we are unmade. We cannot remain the person we were or thought we were. But we are in fact not being destroyed but awakened to the eternally fresh source of our being. We become aware that we are being created, that we are springing from the Creator's hand and returning to Him in love.   —WS 32

Often we are reluctant to admit that we are the sick and sinful whom Jesus came to heal. We prefer our self-protecting isolation to the risk of the face-to-face encounter with the Other in the silence of our vulnerability.   —WS 51

Our center is an open space where the paradoxes of our being are held in dynamic and wonder-filled suspension. Another name for this dynamic suspension of paradox is peace.
                                                          —IC 305

Don't try to use any energy to dispel the distraction. Simply ignore it, and the way to ignore it is to say your word.   —MC

To be silent with another person is truly to be with that other person. Nothing is so powerful in building mutual confidence than an easeful and creative silence. Nothing reveals inauthenticity more dramatically than silence that is not creative but fearful.   —MC

In meditation we declare our own poverty.   —WS 12

The essence of all poverty consists in this risk of annihilation. This is the leap of faith from ourselves to the Other. This is the risk involved in all loving.   —WS 23

Prayer is the great school of community.   —WS

Learning to pray is learning to live as fully as possible in the present moment.   —WS 22

Prayer is the life of the Spirit of Jesus within our human heart: the Spirit through whose anointing we are incorporated into the Body of Christ.   —WS 39

We are praying when we are awakening to the presence of this Spirit in our hearts.   —WS 39

There is no part-time or partial prayer, as if the Spirit were not always alive in our heart. But there are times, our twice-daily meditation, when we make a complete turn of consciousness toward this ever present reality. There comes a level of awakening...when our awareness of this reality is constant throughout the most diverse activities or concerns.   —WS 39

By stillness in the spirit we move in the ocean of God. —IC 338

Our theories can make us impotent and self-important, like people with a car manual but no car.   —IC 329

Real prayer is not our prayer but the prayer of Jesus himself. That prayer is, even now as you read this, flowing in our hearts. Our prayer in this vision is our life force.   —IC 310

The Kingdom of God is not a place but an experience.   —CL

We cannot postpone God.   —WU

God already knows and loves us in our mother's womb. Here, already, is the mystery of silence in which we all share. —WU

We have a principle of unity within our being and it is this — our spirit—which is the image of God within us.   —WS 72

Without spirit there is no productivity, no creativity, no possibility of growth.   —WS 27

There is no way to the truth or to the spirit that is not the way of love. God is love.   —WS 27

The Word proceeds from silence and it returns to the unfathomable silence and limitless love of the Father: the cycle of issuing and returning upon which every lifecycle in creation is based, the cycle in which creation exists at every moment could it but see this with a pure heart.   —WS 33

In the silence of the Word we share his experience of hearing himself eternally spoken by the Father.   —WS 34

Humanity is most Godlike when we give ourselves without measure: when we love. And it is without measure that God gives himself to us.   —WS 46

The language in which we express the spiritual experience changes. The reality of the Spirit does not change.   —WS 50

Meditation expands our knowledge of God because in leading us into self-knowledge it propels us beyond self-consciousness.

—IC 335

We know God to the degree that we forget ourselves. —IC 335

We know God not as an object of our knowledge but by participating in his own self-knowledge, sharing in his life, in his spirit.   —IC 336, St. Irenaeus

Our first step in loving God is to allow ourselves to be loved.

—IC 336

The knowledge God has of himself is one with himself. His self-knowledge is love.   —IC 330

We are called — by name, each personally — into the ocean of oneness that is God.   —PC 112

The really important thing to know in life — for life — is that God is and he is love. It may be of some preparatory use to know also that we are sinners. But it is much more necessary to know, and to know clearly, truthfully, that our sins are of no account. They cannot even exist in the light of his love because they are entirely blotted out, burned away by that pure light.   —IC 309

We learn to look upon and contemplate the Godhead itself and thus to be ourselves divinized.   —WS 20

All religious words point and lead to the silence of a spirit attentive to the presence of God.   —IC 283

The wonder of creation is found not in a succession of awakenings but in the simple all-inclusive awakening of the Son to the
Father.   —WS 35

The Christian is called to see all reality with the eyes of
Christ.   —IC 315

We pay attention to our own true nature, and by becoming fully
conscious of the union of our nature with Christ we become
fully ourselves.   —WS 20

By becoming fully ourselves we enter the fullness of life Jesus
has brought us.   —WS 20

The enduring power of St. Benedict's vision is its humanity.
Often a religious vision of life can lose its human focus, but
for Benedict it is through the humanity of Jesus and our own
humanity that we enter the divine mystery.   —PC

We have to penetrate beyond the surface to make contact with
the new life of the Resurrection.   —IC 312

On this frontier of our identity we are met by a guide who is unlimited consciousness, the person of Jesus Christ. We reach this frontier only if we travel light and if we embrace the one who meets
us with absolute trust. At that moment we know from our own
experience that he is the Way, the Truth, and the Life.   —LH

In his Resurrection and return to the Father, Jesus the man, our
brother, transcended every limitation of his human condition,
the limitations of fear and ignorance no less than those of time
and space.   —WS 37–38

For when the light and kingdom dawn in our hearts, then it touches all we touch. We must not fear the dawn, for the light must dawn and burst and expand in our hearts until it becomes the full dawn of the Resurrection. —IC 324

The building up of the Body of Christ is precisely the consuming desire of Jesus to flood every part of our consciousness with his Spirit. —WS 46

All possible human experience, all reality, has been shot through with Christ's redeeming love. —IC 236

Rooted in this actualized pilgrimage, we know whether anything retards or advances the growth toward completeness in Christ. Does it make us think more about ourselves or less about ourselves? That is the Christian touchstone. —IC 329

As we are unformed he is formed. —IC 338

The first step in personhood is to allow ourselves to be loved. —WS 37

To see himself a person must look at another because the way of selfhood is the way of otherness. —WS 28

By renouncing self we enter the silence and focus upon the other. —WS 60

When we are renouncing self we are in that condition of liberty and receptivity that allows us to be in relationship with the Other. —WS 59

Falling in love is so important because it sweeps us out of ourselves, beyond our limitations, into the reality of the other. —IC 314

As long as our faith is seen as comprising a movement from me to God we can only remain self-centered, earthbound. But in apprehending it as a movement from God to Man we discover ourselves caught up in that movement, in its own depths, self-transcending and returning to the Father through the Son. The Christian name for this movement is Love.   —WS 37

The first step in conversion is allowing ourselves to be loved.
                                                              —IC 308

To love others involves more than thinking of them, more even than enjoying their company, more even than sacrificing ourselves for them; it involves allowing ourselves to be loved by them.   —IC 336

We come to know and love God because we allow him to know and love us. This is the alchemy of love.   —IC

Every personal loving relationship has its source in the movement from lover to beloved, though it has its consummation in a wholly simple communion.   —WS 37

In the superabundance of love we become the person we are called to be.   —WS 45

The tyranny of love is the only true relationship.   —IC 337

The mystery of love is that we become what we delight to gaze upon, and so when we have opened our hearts to his light we become light.   —IC 323

Conversion is commitment to the creativity of love. —IC 307

Our destiny is to find our own insertion point into the cosmic reality of God's love. Only then can we love as he loves because only then can we be who we are.   —IC 308

Just as the roots of trees hold the soil firm and stop erosion, so it is the roots of love that hold the ground of our being together.   —IC 336

Only when we live in and from love do we know that miraculous harmony and integration of our whole being which makes us fully human.   —IC 335

The saint is not superhuman but fully human.   —IC 335

7

Conclusion

To those of you who have recently begun to meditate I would like to send you especially much love and encouragement. The commitment this journey calls from us at first is unfamiliar. It requires faith, perhaps a certain recklessness to begin. But once we have begun, it is the nature of God, the nature of love to sweep us along, teaching us by experience that our commitment is to reality, that our discipline is the springboard to freedom. The fear that the journey is "away from," rather than "toward" is only disproved by experience. This is a journey where ultimately only experience counts. The words or writings of others can add only a little light to the wholly actual, wholly present, and wholly personal reality that lives in your heart and in my heart. Miraculously we can enter this experience together and discover communion and just where communication seemed to break down.

The journey to our own heart is a journey into every heart. And in the first light of the real we see that this is the communion which is the kingdom Jesus was born to establish and in which he is born again in every human heart to realize. What we have left behind is loneliness, confusion, and isolation. What we have found is communion, sureness, and love. Our way is simplicity and fidelity. The simplicity of the mantra. Our fidelity to our daily meditation. As we travel this way we are drawn closer together by the same power of love that unites us.

—PC 40

Bibliography of John Main

Books by John Main

Awakening: On Retreat with John Main. London: Medio Media/Arthur James, 1997.

Christian Meditation: The Gethsemani Talks. London: World Community for Christian Meditation, 1977; Medio Media, 1999.

Community of Love. London: Darton, Longman & Todd, 1990; New York: Continuum, 1999.

The Heart of Creation. London: Darton, Longman & Todd, 1988; New York: Continuum, 1988.

The Inner Christ. London: Darton, Longman & Todd, 1987. Combines *Word into Silence, Moment of Christ, The Present Christ.*

Joy of Being: Daily Readings with John Main. London: Darton, Longman & Todd, 1987; published in the U.S. by Templegate as part of the Modern Spirituality Series.

Letters from the Heart. New York: Crossroad, 1982.

Moment of Christ. London: Darton, Longman & Todd, 1984; New York: Crossroad, 1984.

The Present Christ. London: Darton, Longman & Todd, 1985; New York: Crossroad, 1985.

The Way of Unknowing. London: Darton, Longman & Todd, 1989; New York: Crossroad, 1989.

Word into Silence. London: Darton, Longman & Todd, 1980; New York: Paulist Press, 1981.

Word Made Flesh. London: Darton, Longman & Todd, 1993; New York: Continuum, 1998.

Books about John Main

Freeman, Laurence, O.S.B. *The Life and Teachings of John Main.* London: Medio Media, 2002.

Harris, Paul, ed. *John Main: A Biography in Text and Photos.* London: Medio Media, 2001.

Cassette Tapes

Tapes are available at *www.mediomedia.com.*

Being on the Way.
Christian Meditation: The Essential Teaching.
The Christian Mysteries.
Communitas.
The Door to Silence.
Fully Alive.
In the Beginning.
The Last Conferences.
Word Made Flesh.

THE WORLD COMMUNITY
FOR CHRISTIAN MEDITATION

After John Main's death the seeds of community in the practice of meditation among growing numbers of people around the world began to germinate. There are now meditation groups meeting weekly in more than sixty countries. A quarterly newsletter unites meditators in more than a hundred countries. There are twenty-five Christian Meditation Centres, some with small residential communities. The Community is served by a Guiding Board and an International Centre in London. The annual John Main Seminar and retreats worldwide deepen the journey of meditation for many. A School for Teachers helps people to share the teaching simply and effectively with others.

If you would like to learn more about the community that has grown out of the life and teaching of John Main, you can visit The World Community for Christian Meditation web page at *www.wccm.org* or contact

The World Community for Christian Meditation
International Centre
St. Mark's, Myddelton Square
London EC1R 1XX
Tel: 44 20 7278 2070; Fax: 44 20 7713 6346
E-mail: *mail@wccm.org*

In the United States
The World Community for Christian Meditation
United States National Information Center
15930 N. Oracle Road #196
Tucson, AZ 85739
Tel: 520-825-4325
E-mail: *wccm@mediomedia.com*

MEDIO MEDIA

Medio Media is the publishing arm of the World Community for Christian Meditation. It is committed to the dissemination of the teaching of meditation in the Christian tradition and, in particular, to the work of John Main. It is further committed to the growing dialogue among meditators and seekers of all traditions based on the experience of silence common to all religions.

To obtain a copy of the complete catalog of all Medio Media Christian Meditation resource material, call 1-800-324-8305, or to order and view our complete catalog visit our web site at *www.mediomedia.com*. Contact Medio Media by e-mail at *meditation@mediomedia.com*.

Medio Media Distribution Centers

Medio Media
15930 N. Oracle Road #196
Tucson, AZ 85739
Tel: 520-825-4560

Medio Media
St. Mark's, Myddelton Square
London EC1R 1XX
United Kingdom
Tel: 44 20 7278 2070
E-mail: *mediomedia@wccm.org*